CENTURY 21

By the author of

Nine Roads to Tomorrow
Beyond Tomorrow
The IN *Sports*
Science and Serendipity

YOUR LIFE IN THE

CENTURY 21

YEAR 2001 AND BEYOND

D. S. Halacy, Jr.
Illustrations by Susan Gash

MACRAE SMITH COMPANY : PHILADELPHIA

Library of Congress Catalog Card Number 68-31148
Manufactured in the United States of America

6811

U. S. 1472271

Contents

CENTURY 21

1 Your Life in 2001

It is impossible, of course, for us to know now exactly what kind of life we will lead in the year 2001, but educated guesses indicate that fantastic changes will come about by then. If we could transport someone who lived in 1850 to our world today, his surprise would hardly equal that of one of us similarly set down in the year 2001. Fortunate indeed is the reader now in his teens, for he will be in the prime of life as the twenty-first century begins.

The speed of technological development since the middle thirties has been obvious and dramatic. More of us have television today than had bathtubs then, and it is the same time difference we shall discuss in looking ahead to 2001.

In the 1930s there was no TV, and there were no computers, no radar, no spaceflight and no nuclear energy. Telephones, air-conditioning and even refrigerators were luxury items for most. Frozen foods, credit cards, stereo music, automatic transmissions in automobiles, power lawnmowers and plastics were dreams of the future. Golf was a rich man's sport. A few airline passengers chugged through the air at about 120 miles an hour. Automobiles were not owned by many, and the freeway was known in only a handful of the larger cities. Skindiving, skydiving and water skiing were almost unknown sports. There was no polio vaccine, and anyone who had suggested transplanting a human heart at that time would have been a candidate for the mental hospital. A portable radio could be lifted by a strong man or two small boys, and the transistor was as unheard of as the solar battery. France sat safely behind the Maginot Line, confident that her German enemy would never succeed in breaching it. There were no guided missiles.

Look around us today. An orbiting satellite no longer excites us, and launchings of deep-space craft are routine. Even the prospect of a lunar manned landing is taken pretty much as a matter of course. The transistor personal radio is everywhere, and we have color television smaller than the portable radio of a generation

2

ago. Stereo tape decks are available for car or purse. Credit cards and computers are staging a full-scale revolution in the business and banking world; the computer is also a vital force in science and engineering. Communication is truly global and practically instantaneous.

Extending a straight line from the past to the present and into the future is not a valid way to predict the future; the pace of science and technology quickens at an ever-increasing rate. We must plot a sharply rising curve from now to the year 2001. Conservatively we might estimate about a fourfold increase in scientific and technological developments. With a bit of imagination the sky is surely the limit—a limit extending to the reaches of the solar system and beyond.

There are some pessimists—they prefer to be called realists—who see tragedy for the next generation. We will starve, they claim. We will so befoul the environment that we will sicken and die, or we will use up all of our fuels, minerals and other resources so that civilized life as we know it will be impossible. These dire predictions could, of course, come true. There have been similar predictions in the past. The nineteenth century economist Thomas R. Malthus predicted that man would starve because he was increasing faster than the food supply. When Sir Oliver Lodge later feared that we should run out of fertilizer for continuing the food supply science had provided for the world's growing millions, the German Fritz Haber succeeded in extracting nitrogen from the air, of all places. (Nitrogen has other uses, too, and the Germans mined the sky for explosives during World War I).

We will continue to exploit the great wealth of our

seas, covering most of the earth's surface, and even the wealth beneath the sea bottom. We could take four times as much fish from the sea as we now do, for example. And so we will feed the population even though it grows. As more effective birth control methods become available, the world population most likely will not proliferate as the pessimists fear it will.

We will prospect from orbiting satellites for natural resources. New plants—and perhaps new animals—will be developed. We will mine the sea and the atmosphere, along with the moon and perhaps the planets; nuclear explosive mining will become standard procedure. New biological techniques will be used in processing minerals and other resources. Smog and pollution-abatement will clean up the environment, and conservation techniques will save water and other resources. The desalination of water will be a major effort in 2001. We will change the weather and the climate, perhaps even to modifying the radiation belts about the earth with nuclear explosions. Air conditioning will extend to all outdoors.

Fusion power will solve our problems in this field for the foreseeable future, offering cheap and abundant electricity from sea water. We will be able to beam that energy all over the world without wires and even send it into space to power probes and satellites. There will be a shift to electric power, using new converters like the fuel cell, MHD (magnetohydrodynamics), thermionics, and thermoelectricity. Nuclear energy will provide half of this electricity by 2001, and power generation through nuclear explosion may come about. Dwindling fossil fuels will still be important, so lesser grade deposits will be exploited through new techniques.

For a world more than ever on the go, personal transportation will continue to be the automobile. Electric power will supersede the gasoline engine for reasons of economy, environmental purity, noise factors, and simplicity. Vertical takeoff fixed-wing aircraft will largely supersede helicopters and other rotary-wing types. Air cars will serve over water and rough terrain. Trains will ride on a thin cushion of air at 300-mile-an-hour speeds. In the air the SST (supersonic transport) will be followed by the HST (hypersonic transport), capable of five thousand miles per hour and faster. By 2001 we will be colonizing the planets, in addition to the moon.

We may communicate with each other telepathically, and we will have machines that are intelligent. The English language will be a world language, and all the world will be tied together by what would seem to us today a fantastic electronic network. Three great "super cities" will dominate the United States—one on the east coast, one on the west coast, and another in the Great Lakes region. World harmony will be insured by computer planning of economic developments. Voting will be done from the home by computer. We will live longer and healthier lives in 2001. We may alter our bodies genetically for the better and we may spend part of our lives in cryogenic suspended animation. Prenatal care and treatment will eliminate most congenital defects. Mental illness will be controlled, as will physical problems such as obesity. Sleep machines will provide more restful relaxation and dreams may be "programed" for the same reason. Medical care will be given to all, and emergency techniques will be improved so that few accidental deaths occur. The population will be controlled by improved birth control methods; the sex of babies will be determined or even chosen before birth. We will beautify our physique, complexion, hair and features safely and cheaply. Replacement of vital organs and of limbs will be commonplace. Hearing and vision will be artificially extended, and memory and learning ability in humans and animals will be improved with drugs.

Television, radio and the home computer will provide instantaneous communication with the rest of the world through satellite links. The "pocket pager" will connect the individual to this network so that even from remote areas he can communicate, have the use of a computer, and so on. Mail, shopping service, library research, and news services will be electronic. And of course the vidiphone will let us see and be seen as we talk to someone.

The computer, global communication, the teaching machine, and business and industry will play a great part in education in 2001. Teaching-machine techniques will insure that students learn faster and more thoroughly. TV will bring the world to the classroom, and business and industry will provide for new employees the upper years of their schooling.

Programed learning, sleep teaching and speech compression will seem old-fashioned compared with memory- and learning-enhancement through drugs. It may be possible to improve the reasoning capability of the mind with drugs, electronic stimulation or direct attachment to computers.

With far more leisure time—and money—in 2001, we may witness a remarkable change in our identities. We may be known for our avocation rather than what we do for a livelihood—mountain-climber instead of welder, for example, or lunar explorer instead of computer analyst. High-speed transportation will greatly change the vacation pattern, and trips around the world will be made for weekend jaunts, or even in one day. Most of our present sports will continue, and a few new ones may be added. Air and water sports will increase, particularly that of skindiving. For some, TV will continue to fill leisure hours. Others will find diversion in the "Disneylands" and "Las Vegases" that will spring up about the country. The most exciting avocation will be lunar travel, or even interplanetary voyages.

Business will not be as usual in 2001. Man will have learned that he is not doomed to go through life making marks on paper, and executives, managers, secretaries and even clerks will lead more interesting and rewarding lives at work. "Voice writers" will take dictation, and computer-linked printouts will do the chores that face today's stenographer. The average income for a family of four will approach $50,000, yet there will be little money handled. Record keeping and data processing will be done on and by computers. In fact, the computer will pervade life in 2001. Coupled with automation to produce "cybernation," it will produce our goods and run our stores. It will do the data processing for business, schools, libraries and government. Science and engineering will rely heavily on the computer to make tremendous and rapid advances in all fields. Our homes will also be run by electronic computer "housekeepers" and tended by robot servants.

Science and engineering will give us new uses for recent developments like the laser and maser. There will be new industrial materials, including metals, ceramics, "cermets" (ceramic-metallic combinations), plastics, cloths, and papers. The just-discovered miracle of "holography" will make possible photographs, illustrations, TV and moving pictures in three dimensions.

There is a most vital factor we have not yet considered, and that is the importance of spiritual and moral values in the world of 2001. Materially the world will have advanced a great deal, but real progress for humanity will be measured in how wisely we can use such blessings. Basic values do not change. Just as the law of gravity will hold, so will the laws of human conduct: faith, hope, and love, honesty, trust, kindness and loyalty.

A huge Gross National Product will not necessarily expand the size of men's hearts; the fact that we can circumnavigate the globe in five or six hours and fly to the moon in two days will make us no wiser and no more spiritually mature. But neither should they make us any less compassionate or intelligent. The key point is that in 2001, no less than today, it will be love that truly makes the world go round. There is reason to hope that men who are well fed and sounder in body and mind will devote more of their leisure time to noble purposes.

It is also true that we could blow up the world ourselves between now and 2001, of course, but most likely we won't. The sun could explode, or a wandering chunk of celestial rock miles in diameter could slam into the earth and demolish it, but neither of these catastrophes is likely. Disease, earthquakes or tidal waves could kill us all, but the odds are greatly against such an end. Instead, the chances are excellent that you will be alive and well in 2001 and that life in the twenty-first century will be wonderful. In the chapters that follow we will see just how interesting and different a life it will be.

2 Home, Sweet Home

Your home in 2001 will much resemble the one you would *like* to live in today—from the outside, that is. Inside it will be much more elegant and advanced than the most sophisticated automated home now available. Many of the technical and architectural features that will be standard in 2001 have already been designed or suggested. For the homeowner of the future they will come so gradually that the difference will not be obvious. But to us, looking in suddenly on the expected effects of the decades of progress, the result will seem startlingly wonderful.

As we approach the front door, it opens silently, triggered by the "key" in our pocket. In case a visitor approached, the door would not open, but a bell or chime would ring inside to announce the arrival. Should no one be home, the bell would not sound and a computer message would inform the caller. Incidentally, sensing devices would actuate burglar alarms or other defense mechanisms if someone tried to break in or harm the house. A direct tie-in with the police will insure that help will soon be at hand.

The door swings shut behind us and music begins to play softly from speakers throughout the house. As we move from room to room the lights come on if needed, actuated by sensors. Of course we can override these controls and turn the lights from full off to full on with handily located touch switches. Instead of fixtures in the ceiling, or lamps in the corner, the walls and ceilings themselves glow with soft light almost like that of daytime. It may, in fact, be daylight, stored in luminescent panels and saved for use later.

As newcomers from earlier times we notice the spotless floor coverings in all the rooms. Whether tile, plastic or cloth carpet, they all appear to have just been cleaned. Indeed, this is the case. The thick carpet in the living room is an endless belt of material that revolves at night and is cleaned chemically for the next day's use.

The tile floors and polished furniture are a housewife's dream: there is not a speck of dust visible. Electrostatic precipitators are part of the reason, electric charges attracting the particles of dust. There are electrostatic filters in the air-conditioning system, and automatic floor cleaners and vacuum sweepers that operate silently while the residents sleep.

Entire walls in some rooms are of glass, but of a kind of glass we have never seen before. In place of drapes, varying patterns form and disappear, caused by electron beams through the glass itself, which is in effect a thin color TV tube. As a matter of fact, when we are ready to watch a movie or the news, a wall becomes a life-size screen for full-sound, full-color, three-dimensional entertainment. A feature of outside glass walls and all windows in the house is their ability to darken automatically and shut out glare from bright sun. At night, a similar property makes them opaque for privacy.

Most rooms are equipped with TV screens, plus speakers for music, which may be from radio stations, the home tape library, or "random" music composed by the home computer.

In our time the lady of the house goes to the freezer and the pantry and processes the food stored there in her stove or oven. In 2001 the meal center will do that job for her. Programed by computer with instructions for the homemaker (overridden once in a while by the youngsters or husband for a change of diet) or from the clinic, the food center selects the desired packaged foods and heats or chills them along with beverages to complement the meal. Assembled, the entire meal is held at a service center until the family is ready to eat. Wheeled to the table, it is served. When the meal is finished, everything goes back into the service center and dishes and utensils are automatically washed, sterilized and returned to their proper places—or disposed of, if they are expendable items, of which there will be many.

Incidentally, although there will be a refrigerator for ice and a few items desired to be kept cold for better taste, today's familiar freezer will be nowhere in sight. Irradiation by penetrating rays will keep meat, vegetable, and other foods fresh on the shelf at room temperature for weeks and even months.

In our time the automatic dishwasher has been joined by the automatic oven cleaner that automatically burns itself gleaming bright. By 2001 the bathtub will have joined this automatic parade, and the ring about the tube will be no concern either of the bather who makes it or of the one who follows him. It will automatically be sprayed, brushed or scraped off. Or maybe the tub will have a disposable plastic liner that will peel off and rinse down the drain!

In the patio we will find a lawn that looks like the real thing although the homeowner does not boast a green thumb and hasn't the time to do the yard-work required by living things. The lawn is an outside carpet —of green or of whatever color appeals to the taste. Flowers, shrubs and even trees are artificial, although we must look closely to realize this. Air conditioning extends outdoors too, so that if nature serves up a day that is too hot or too cold the temperature and humidity can be regulated at will. The advantages of this artificial yard are apparent: no watering chores, no crabgrass and no blisters. For the avid gardener, however, real landscaping will be available. He will take advantage of such aids as automatic underground irrigation (to save evaporation losses and keep his yard dry for recreation at all times), and plastic covers and reflectors to reduce moisture loss and increase sunshine intake.

The house we are visiting is in the suburbs and receives its electricity in a different way than those in urban areas, where a central power station provides electricity through underground wires. Situated in an area of much sunshine, this home is solar heated and solar powered. Part of its roof and some of the outside walls consist of movable panels of reflective or insulating material. These are moved during the day and night, silently and automatically, to let in or keep out sunshine (which includes heat, of course). A pond of water in the attic stores heat for use during cloudy weather or at nighttime when heat is needed. In summer, heat is radiated away from the pond to the cool night sky and keeps the inside temperature at a pleasant level. Standby electrical refrigeration operates automatically when needed, using solar-generated electricity. Part of the roof is "shingled" with solar cells. With a conversion efficiency of about ten percent, these provide ample current to storage batteries or fuel cells to take care of all the power needs of the house.

In areas where there is not sufficient sunshine, or where an owner hasn't such modern ideas, a central power plant in the form of a fuel cell will do the job. Operating on kerosene, fuel oil or gasoline, perhaps filled from the tank of the family car, this plant is silent and has no moving parts. Designed to last as long as the house, it is fireproof, foolproof and economical. There will be no outside wires to this home for utilities, and blackouts from power failures will be a thing of the past and no worry to the self-sufficient homeowner.

A small power plant in the utility room does not mean that the home of 2001 will not require large quantities of power. It will. What we call a total electric home today will seem quite primitive by the new standards. Take the home computer, for example. Beginning in the 1960s, some families have had the advantage of a computer terminal in their homes. Dad could figure his engineering problems or proposed investments with the aid of a central computer many miles away. Mom enlisted the computer to take care of the bank account and even recipes. And the youngsters got help with math homework and other problems with the home computer terminal. By 2001 the home will be *run* by the computer. Let's see how it will do this.

Suppose you live in a neighborhood that still gets power from a plant some distance away. The electric meter will be fed directly to the computer, which will relay readings to a central billing agency. A tie-in with the meal center maintains an inventory of food in the pantry, printing out a shopping list for Mom each week, or perhaps only every two weeks. Money, in the form of bills and change, will have little use. Instead, financial affairs will be carried on by computers. But when Dad wants to, he can interrogate the home computer and see his bank balance at any time—also, how much he owes on the house, the car, and any other purchases the family has made.

The computer will run the housecleaning equipment, control air conditioning and lighting, and program music, news and television entertainment for the family. In this last application it may even arbitrate and work out amicable compromises when various members want to view more TV programs simultaneously than there are TV receivers in the home!

Let's research a term paper using the home computer. We interrogate the library, asking for a particular subject. Five minutes later the teleprinter rattles off several hundred lines of data and adds an extensive bibliography, in case we need more information. Some of the material was on hand at the library in town; some came from the Library of Congress; but some came from other places, too, including files of newspapers, government agencies in seven countries, and libraries on three continents.

In addition, the computer also prints out the news on a TV screen every hour, (or on paper if we desire), with stock market reports, weather, merchandise sales, and so on. It reminds us, either in writing or verbally, of appointments, important dates, errands to run, shopping to do, and so on.

Although the house we are imagining does not resemble any of the others in the neighborhood, it was factory built as a prefabricated series of units and simply assembled on the building site. This particular model was delivered the twenty miles from the factory by helicopter crane in three modules. It is of steel where structural strength is needed, and a combination of cement and synthetic materials. The structure is stressed to withstand the sonic booms we hardly notice by now, even from the Mach 8 aircraft that fly overhead. The house will also withstand a fairly close nuclear blast and the subsequent fallout in case this should ever happen. The windows automatically darken to shut out penetrating radiation and heat, as we saw earlier. There is ample food and water for a month in case the family is isolated for that long. And of course the power supply will continue to function so that radio and television are received and computer contact is maintained. Needless to say, the house is fireproof. It is also windproof against even a tornado and designed to withstand all but the worst earthquakes. It is tidy, too, and in dry weather periodically washes its exterior for appearance's sake.

With the shorter work week of 2001, there will be much more leisure time, and so the leisure room—or game room, or rumpus room, as it was once called—will be important. There will still be the ubiquitous pool and Ping-Pong tables, but these will be better designed for quick and easy storage. The leisure room may be fitted with sliding partitions to make it two or more smaller rooms so that several activities can go on at once. These partitions will be acoustically treated for silence, of course. The computer may well get into the recreation act too and you'll play chess, checkers or other games with it. Unless it is programed for defeat only a master player will win against the machine, however. Fairer will be chess matches played via the computer with human opponents across the nation or around the world. Where such games once required correspondence for each move and were enjoyed by only a few, any fan in 2001 can take advantage of such recreation on a global basis. In a later chapter we shall go more fully into leisure activities of the future.

Evolution of Tomorrow's Home

While there have been predictions of future cities in which humans will live like rabbits in a warren or bees in a hive, some emerging psychological truths argue against this kind of "packaging" of people. Overcrowding leads to increases in crime and to psychological breakdowns. So, besides the esthetic reason, there is another very good one against the compact apartment in the compact, skyscraper tenement.

The power homes of today are nevertheless better than many of those of a century or more ago. Improvements due to technology and living standards will increase by 2001, and while there will be "slums," we will not recognize them as such on our visit to the future.

The average home of 2001 will generally be smaller, for the very good reason that families will be smaller by then. Most families will be planned, and the goal will be simply to replace oneself instead of being part of a world-crowding population explosion. As a result, homes will have fewer bedrooms and bathrooms.

Along with planned families will be planned neighborhoods, villages and cities. Begun in the 1950s in such places as Reston, Virginia, and Rancho Bernardo, California, recreationally planned communities will gain in popularity. Instead of rows and rows of equi-spaced blocks of houses and streets, the model village will have gently curving roads, bicycle and walking paths, and access to schools, churches and recreation without need for the family car. Freeways will be screened from residential areas but will be easily accessible for the trip to the city for work.

Early in man's history he lived in homes that lasted practically forever. When he forsook caves for houses he gained some features but lost the longevity he was accustomed to. The lifetime of a home has decreased, for a variety of reasons, and now it is common to calculate it at about forty years. This means, of course, that most of the homes of 2001 will not have been built in 1968.

It is possible that in 2001 we shall be living in "igloos" made of special plastics, or in apartments bored into solid rock, the better to resist atomic attack. Conceivably we might be living in homes built over a body of water instead of on solid ground. It is not probable that home life will be like this, however. In spite of recent model "cities of the future" looking like clusters of shoeboxes stuck together in a disordered pile, the homes of the future will not be revolutionarily different from those we spend our days and nights in now.

In 1930 the author lived in a more or less typical house of that period. It was built of wood, with a shingle roof, and had electricity and gas utilities. It was fenced and had trees in the backyard. Underneath was an ancient and unused cistern, which had once held water for domestic use, but there was inside plumbing, with hot and cold running water. There was a gas cook stove in the kitchen, and portable kerosene stoves heated the rest of the house.

The uninspired floor plan consisted of a living-room, a dining-room, a kitchen, several bedrooms, and a bathroom. The house was laid out in "streetcar" fashion, one room behind another, with a hall down one side. Landscaping, except for the sparse lawn and trees in the back, was nonexistent. Mainly this was so because the house itself fronted on the sidewalk, with room only for a narrow border of grass and a few geraniums. Today the house would qualify perhaps as an upper-middle slum, although at the time it seemed nice enough.

Planwise, the author's present home differs mainly in that it is a single-story residence and has a more imaginative floor plan with bedrooms in a wing, plus large sliding glass doors facing the back yard. The landscaping, too, is more imaginative, with a large front yard (it seems too large when the grass must be mowed!), trees, flowers and shrubs. The backyard too is large, with many trees, a lawn, and flowers. However, the house design itself is basically little different from that of nearly four decades ago. It is built of cement block, to be sure, and is well insulated and air conditioned. The windows are larger, as are the rooms themselves. But the rooms are still rectangular in shape, the house has square corners, and the pitched roof looks much as roofs have looked for centuries.

In short, the wild-eyed predictions that filled the popular mechanics magazines and the Sunday sections of the newspapers have not materialized. Homes of the future, if we were to believe some writers of the thirties, would be pneumatic, inflated like balloons for simplicity and economy. Furniture, too, would be air-filled. Or, if you believed another school, we would all live in trailers before long. Neither of these predictions, nor any of the other visionary ideas, has come to pass for the average home-dweller. We still live in houses with walls and roofs, doors and windows. Yes, and even fireplaces in some instances. The big changes in homes over the past thirty-five to forty years has been an improvement in a basic design. The average home today is larger, roomier, more comfortable. (We are not talking now of homes of the very rich, for there is a tendency in the top income bracket to build much smaller homes than the Astors and Vanderbilts and Rockefellers once erected as near-monuments to themselves.)

Homes today are more livable and more comfortable and offer more features and conveniences. Today's residence has much more "house-power" than did that of 1930—at least the one this writer lived in. In those days the electric bill was small, but it bought only lighting, a radio, (usually), washing machine (sometimes) and refrigerator (less often). Today electricity provides light, radio, high-fi, television, washer, dryer, refrigerator, freezer, refrigeration for the home, pumps for pools, and often range and oven, which were once gas-fired or even wood-burning.

The home of the future, in most cases, will not be a revolutionary departure from that of today. While some *may* live in boxlike skyscrapers or on rafts or in trees, most of us will dwell in residences that from the outside may not look greatly different from the more advanced homes being built now. But there will be a tremendous difference inside. Once man spent much of his time in caring for his house. The trend is in the opposite direction—our homes in the future will care for us!

As the business week and the work week shrink, the housewife will want a similar lessening of her duties so that she too can enjoy the extra leisure. Also, working wives will be more common, and this too will demand homes that require less hours spent on them by their occupants.

The mark of success in times past has often been the

number of slaves—and later, servants—a family possessed. The slaves were freed, and fewer and fewer people worked as servants. This is a powerful motivating force for the production of robot help for the house. The home of 2001 will be even more servantless than ever, in fact it will be only the very well off who can find and pay personal servants such as maids, cooks and housekeepers.

Some might argue that this will not be good; that man will not profit by becoming so "lazy." It helps to think back or read the history books and learn that once it was necessary to go out, cut down a tree, saw stove lengths, split kindling, build a wood fire, and tend it carefully to cook a meal. Surely today we enjoy the meal as much or maybe more for getting it more easily. Of course, an occasional stint of picnicking or camping out is fun and good for the soul and conscience. But nobody can seriously argue for a steady diet of such labor. Beating the rugs may be remembered with eye-misting emotion by some, but the vacuum cleaner does a better job all around. When the vacuum cleaner runs itself, who will complain?

3 Government

In 2001 there will be three hundred million people in the United States. We will still be a republic, governed by a President and a Congress. But much will be different, besides the fact that we are half again as large in population as we were in the late 1960s. One such difference, and perhaps the most noticeable, will be the "super-cities." There will be three of these.

"BosWash" will dominate the northeast, a huge metropolitan area with a population of seventy-five million. As its name indicates, it will extend generally from Boston, Massachusetts, to Washington, D. C., with considerable overlap, including Maine in the northeast and Virginia to the south. Reaching great distances back from the coastline, BosWash will include about one-fourth of the country's population and will be the most politically powerful of the supercities.

To the west will be the second largest megalopolis, "ChiPitts" (or "Pittsicago," as it is sometimes humorously called). This huge manufacturing area will center around the Great Lakes and be populated by about forty-five million Americans.

A greater distance to the west we will find sprawling "SanSan," largest in physical size of the three complexes, although it is still smallest in numbers with almost thirty million inhabitants. SanSan will have the distinction of being the only city entirely within what was once one state, and its mayor will also be governor of both the Californias. Southern and Upper. SanSan will extend from the Mexican border at San Diego to San Francisco.

Roughly half the entire population will live in the great cities of BosWash, ChiPitts, and SanSan, then. It would seem that these great city-states would control the nation, and indeed they would, except for the constant jockeying between and among them for power. Generally, ChiPitts and SanSan will join together to prevent BosWash (bigger than both of them) from ruling. This gives the remainder of the nation, living mostly in suburban and rural areas with a concentration about what it was nationwide in the 1960s, all the chance it needs to assure itself fair representation in government affairs. However, as the outskirts of Bos-Wash and ChiPitts creep ever closer together, the day will come when these two giants merge (although perhaps against the wishes of the mayors then in office!). Their combined strength of about 120 million may result in national political control.

Except in SanSan, the governors of the included states will be subservient to the mayor. Outside the "megalopoli" the other states will function much as they did decades earlier except for administrative improvements and other changes that have been made. Let's take a look at a small state in the West.

Arizona is fortunate or unfortunate, depending on one's viewpoint, in not being close enough to qualify for membership in SanSan. Long stretches of desert, as well as some mountains, buffer her from California. While its population will double to four million, Arizona will still be one of the smallest states in the nation with respect to population. Although its major cities of Phoenix and Tucson will practically merge into a slender complex bordering the connecting freeway, they will retain their identities. This may be true only because neither "Tunix" or "Phoeson" has the right megalopolitan ring!

Local government will change little in Arizona. As we shall see, the situation is different in the large cities, but let's pursue things at the level of the outlying states first. Councils function with a mayor to give direction to the professional managers who actually operate the business of the city or town. In the Capitol a 120-man legislature (forty senators and eighty representatives), makes the state's laws. It will sit in session twice a year, for three months each session, and do research and interim committee work in the months between. For this civic duty each legislator will be paid what he earned in the last year of his previous employment, plus a standard yearly incremental increase. No legislator will serve for more than two four-year terms.

Court officials will be selected by a board and serve one term. The governor will be elected for four years, appoint his own cabinet, and serve only one term, subject to recall after serving half of that. Law enforcement will be rigid but with ample safeguards against unfair punishment. The public defender has his counterpart in the *ombudsman* who protects the interests of private citizens who feel they are being unfairly treated by local government.

Old-fashioned lapel-button, handshaking electioneering has nearly vanished from the political scene. Campaigning is done almost entirely by television, with equal time guaranteed to all who are qualified to run in the general elections. Voting in local issues will be done by computer from the home, as it will be for all elections. A major difference is that all ballots are cast nearly simultaneously, with the vote tally held in the computer all during the day of elections, then printed out the moment the polls close. This will give no chance for results of voting across the country to affect a local vote. The nearly hundred-percent voting record will seem amazing until we learn that voting became a civic must ten years ago. Unjustified failure to vote will lead to a sizable fine and compulsory attendance at civics classes. Voting, incidentally, will be legal at age 19.

In line with the historic "one man, one vote" rulings

handed down by the courts in earlier days, the Electoral College will no longer exist. The President will be elected by popular vote. Mayors will be elected during the "off" years—that is, two years before or after the President, along with governors.

There has recently been fear on the part of many states that the cities would completely bypass them and deal directly with the Federal government in Washington. In 2001 this will not have happened. In the outlying areas, city and state governments will work well together, both retaining much of the money once paid in taxes to Washington. With BosWash, ChiPitts, and SanSan, however, the situation will be even further from the fears of a few decades ago. The cities will to a large extent bypass the states, but they will bypass Uncle Sam as well! The three supercities will collect the bulk of taxes in their areas and provide most of the services. Their mayors will have near-cabinet rank and meet often with the President to coordinate the affairs of the country.

There will still be two major political parties and a handful of minor ones that come and go. The democratic process and representative government will prevail; in fact it will be more democratic and more representative, thanks in large part to new methods of communication between elected representatives and the constituency they represent.

The computer will be the most powerful tool for better government, just as it is for better business, education, weather prediction, space travel, or any other field. Computer runs demonstrate the feasibility of proposed government programs, calculate the amount of taxation necessary, and predict future needs of the country and the world. The computer aids the regular election process but has another big advantage. In addition to the political elections held every two years, informal but highly important polls will be taken each week—sometimes each day—on topical issues. Where straw votes tallied by newspapers or private and not always ethical pollsters once had to serve, it will be possible to put an electronic finger on the pulse of the nation's voters—each of them, actually!—and make a decision that will be the wish of the majority.

To the argument that people don't know what is good for them, proponents of computer polling will answer "If they don't who does?" While there are of course selfish, shortsighted people who would wreck things for their own advantage, a majority of the people can generally be counted on to make the right decision. Indeed, there will be half-serious suggestions that the voting public no longer needs representatives in the state capital or in Washington, since they now exercise their voting right individually on practically every issue that comes up. However, this further refinement, if it really is that, will take a little longer to work out.

Crime will remain a problem in 2001, but not nearly to the extent that it was earlier. Much of the credit for reducing crime will go to the medical profession and to those lay citizens concerned enough to make it possible for the doctors to do what was needed. Medical testing beginning with birth and continued through the school years, plus counseling and a close check of records, will identify those who are criminally inclined for organic reasons. The correctable will be treated; those beyond help will be isolated so that they cannot harm society but still be permitted a useful, constructive life.

With the bulk of dangerous criminals taken care of humanely, law-enforcement officers will have more time to handle the still frequent occurrences of crime. All people who break the law are not medically prone to do so; any of us is likely to make a mistake now and then. Fair but firm treatment will generally limit such offenses to one per person.

A particularly effective technique will require service by every male citizen in law enforcement or the military. Such stints in uniform generally instill much respect for career officers. In addition to being highly skilled, carefully selected, and well-paid, the law officer of 2001 will have the citizenry almost solidly behind him.

The World in 2001

There will be three hundred million people in the United States in 2001, as noted earlier. There will be six billion in all the world.

Surprisingly, there will have been little consolidation among nations in the last several decades. The only notable example will be Greater Europe, comprising nations of the old Common Market. Even this will be a loose federation, with most members still retaining strong national feelings.

The United Nations will have celebrated its first fifty years not too long ago, a surprise to those who feared it could not endure the agonizing problems that constantly beset such an organization. But it will no longer be in the United States, since it was felt wise to share this honor with other nations. Currently the head-quarters will be in Australia, where a huge complex of buildings housing the United Nations will be turned over to that country in 2005 for use by its own government. The next home of the United Nations will be Liberia. Thus, within a century, some twenty nations will have the privilege of hosting the organization.

Even with the headquarters many thousands of miles away from Washington, our government will be in instant contact with the United Nations. It will also have "cold lines" (rather than the original hot lines set up years ago) to all the major powers in the form of TV satellite relays. There is daily communication by world leaders in this way without the time, expense, and slight risk involved in air travel for conferences.

Although there will have been several small incidents and even a couple that might be called wars in recent years, the nightmare of global war will not have come by 2001. Perhaps it never will. One of the greatest assurances in this regard will be the giant peace-keeping computer complex strung all around the world, with its master console in Sydney. Put quite simply, and over the objections of the many proud humans involved, the job of keeping the world safe for democracy and whatever other forms of government are favored in various countries will be taken over by machines—in this case, electronic analysts and referees.

A computer can do just about anything it is told to do if enough facts are fed into it. The peacekeeper will be told to maintain peace by keeping the world healthy, well-fed, and happy, and to do this it will be linked with indicators of business, weather, agriculture, politics, population, and other pertinent factors in the world. There was a time when a computer that could reserve you a seat in the first class section of Flight 110 from New York to Lisbon on the 4th of next March was hailed as a miracle. "Peacekeeper" can—and will—tell everybody how many nuclear spacecraft Greater Europe has, the size of America's standing army, and the caloric intake of the poorest peasants in Asia. It will allocate cotton acreage for a farmer in Louisiana and tell parents in Greenland that they may have another child next year without paying a tax on their family. The computer will predict a warm spell for Albania late in the year, and the weather control station nearest that country will program a weather modification effort for those two weeks. That's election time and no one wants tempers frayed by soaring thermometers!

Some will balk at orders issued by "Peacekeeper"—the American boatbuilder, for instance, told to stop producing a certain model for export; and the Dutch fuel cell plant ordered to change to another line of business. But in the years that follow they and the rest of the world will prosper as they would not have otherwise. The computer will be programed to do just that. The best results for everyone concerned is what it will strive for. The proper specialization in manufacturing, efficient agricultural effort, the correct birth rate. It will work. It will work so well that most of the time nobody will even think about it. Fears that it would be subverted by representatives of one country or bloc will prove wrong, since the global computer will have no axe to grind and there will be little danger of someone trying to take an axe to *it*. Not that such a saboteur would get far. The computer will be carefully guarded against such an attack. It will also have duplicate "brains" all over the world!

Unfortunately, computers will not eliminate armies and weapons. For too many centuries men have had to rely on war as a method of guarding their interests. Suppose Peacekeeper somehow fell into the wrong hands? Suppose an enemy attacked without alerting the monitors stationed around the world to guard against such a thing's happening? Suppose . . . ? So every major power retains an army and weapons that make those of past wars seem toys.

Included in this arsenal of 2001 will be laser death rays that can knock incoming nuclear warheads out of the sky at thousand-mile range; weather machines to flood or scorch out an enemy; and tidal-wave producers that will drown his population. The latest bomb will be the "antimatter" device whose horrible implosion produces blasts that will make the hydrogen bomb a popgun by comparison. Radiation and chemical warfare will be developed and ready to make corpses or living dead of fighting men and civilians alike. The most insidious weapons of all will be deadly drugs that can be introduced into a water supply to turn the population into helpless zombies who willingly cooperate in their own destruction. All of these, of course, only argue the stronger for Peacekeeper and more of its kind. And since the computer approach to world peace is more likely to work than any man-governed scheme, most citizens will rest easy in their beds for having seen the latest report from the big screen in Sydney.

Despite the fact that the computer is everywhere part of government, the system in 2001 will be one that Abraham Lincoln can still be proud of. His government "of the people, by the people, for the people" will not have perished from the face of the earth, which is a tribute to him and to most of the leaders who have followed.

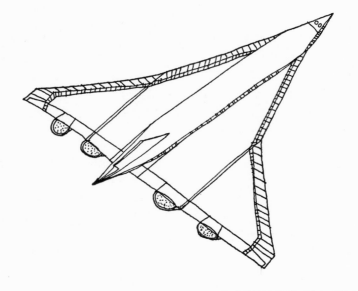

4 Transportation

There is a story to the effect that every American owns two automobiles—and drives both of them at once. Certainly we are a nation on the go, and nobody ever seems to be where he wants to be. Transportation is a major factor in our lives; it will be even more so in 2001.

Man once traveled on "shank's mare," that is, on his

own two legs. Later the horse was domesticated and was the favorite means of transportation. Shortly after the turn of the twentieth century the automobile began to supplant the faithful four-footed beast of burden, although scoffers advised pioneer automobilists in their goggles and dusters to "get a horse!" It was the horse that finally lost out, relegated to pasture, race track and Western movie. The automobile will remain the most popular method of transportation in 2001, but it will look about as much like the cars we drive today as those resemble designs of 1930.

In one respect the new cars will be similar to the antiques that occasionally move noiselessly along our streets nowadays; they will be powered by electricity. Decades ago the electric car was popular. One was driven across the country in the days when that was a remarkable feat for any form of transportation. But silent battery power lost out to the ravenous gasoline engine. Only the growing menace of smog put the electric car back into the running, although it has many additional benefits beyond its smog-free operation.

Our electric automobile of 2001 will be compact and simple in design. It will be quiet and smooth in operation, with no clashing of gears, yet it will accelerate as fast as present cars and travel at a higher top speed. The electric motor needs no cooling system, ignition, carburetion, muffler, gears or clutch. It will have four individual motors, one driving each wheel directly. Brakes will be electromagnetic, with the useful ability to charge the batteries when applied!

When we think of an electric car we visualize batteries to drive it. Some cars will use this form of power, but the fuel cell will most likely be favored for its high

U. S. 1472271

efficiency and for the fact that it eliminates the need for recharging. The fuel cell is filled just like a gas tank—perhaps can be filled even with gasoline by 2001 —and converts the liquid directly to electricity, which operates motors and accessories. But let's see what happens when we leave the city streets and swing onto the freeway of 2001 with our electric car.

The term *auto*mobile will have new meaning as we "latch on" to the gleaming metal strip in the lane we have selected. At the proper speed we flip a switch on the dash and go on automatic. Now even the driver can sit back and relax as electronic controls monitor our speed and see to it that we turn at the proper ramps to reach the destination we set on the panel selector. Although we are not rigidly attached to the track, and can override the automatic system at any time we want, electronic guidance steers us surely along the track, negotiating the sweeping curves of the freeway more smoothly than we could do it ourselves. Distance from the next car ahead is maintained by a central traffic computer, with the additional safeguard of an emergency radar probe that brakes us safely in case we get too close. Should someone overtake us and approach too close, an automatic warning system alerts us to the danger.

Normally we will drive at the maximum speed of a hundred miles an hour; but when changing ramps, or if we want to do some leisurely sightseeing, we can change lanes, automatically or under manual control. Although it is not legal for the driver of a car on the freeway to sleep, tests have been conducted in which a *driverless* car traveled safely from BosWash to SanSan nonstop in twenty-four hours. In spite of this demonstration of the foolproof automatic highway, there will be the standard jokes about the little old lady from ChiPitts who got on the Loop on a vacation trip and starved to death before the highway patrol came to her rescue.

Early electric cars were severely restricted in range because of the weight and size of batteries. How can we drive nonstop clear across the country? It's easy when the power comes from the freeway itself. The guidance strip functions like the old "third rail" of the streetcar, furnishing not only electronic control signals but power for the motor as well. But before you get the idea that this is free power, let's point out that computers record your license number and bill your account automatically for your trip!

A bonus of the automatic freeway will be the drastic reduction in highway fatalities. Even the drunken driver will find it difficult to cause an accident in 2001. If he should override the automatic controls and veer all over the freeway, automatic sensing equipment on other cars protects them from trouble. About the only accidents that occur will involve two drunk drivers: poetic justice on wheels.

Let's take a look at the car itself. It is about the size of present-day compacts, but more "futuristic." There is a huge plastic bubble instead of a metal top, formed of a variable-opacity material that darkens automatically against sun glare. Inside are reclining seats, stereo music, stereo color TV, plus a snack bar with a small refrigerator for pleasant long trips. Radiophones are standard equipment for two-way communication with office, home, or anywhere. Again, calls are automatically billed against your account.

It seemed that everybody owned two cars back in the 1960s. Surprisingly, in 2001 many people won't own even one electric car. They will just rent them when needed and will find the service excellent.

As the saying goes, wheels must be popular; they've been 'round for about 6,000 years. They will still be 'round in 2001 and our small personal electric cars will run on them. Of course there will be small air-cars, or hovercraft, but these are used mostly for rough terrain, or overwater trips. Ancient as it is, the good old wheel remains tried and true, particularly when it is of solid material and can't blow out. In 2001 all streets and freeways will be so smooth that pneumatic tires are a thing of the past except for the few antiques licensed to operate as curiosities.

Try the Train!

A cruising speed of a hundred miles an hour is adequate, but on the freeway we will notice another form of transportation that makes us think our car has gone into reverse. Riding tiered tracks in the median strip, airtrains will zoom along at a scheduled speed of three hundred miles an hour, crossing the country in eight hours nonstop, or in about ten hours with stops in large cities along the way. A combination of monorail and the air-cushion principle, the trains will race along on a cushion of air about a half-inch thick. When they slow for stops, the runners will settle down on small wheels at a speed of about a hundred miles an hour. These wheels are motor-driven to get the train moving, but at liftoff speed propulsion shifts to electromagnetic drive. Huge coils encircle the four tracks at intervals and the induced field hurtles the train along at its breathtaking rate. Speed with safety will be the motto, and there will be few accidents.

In the cities there will be trains that race through tunnels bored deep in the ground. Some of these are pneumatic trains, "fired" through the tunnels like shells in a gun barrel. Not very scenic, but a quick way to get across town. Most travelers prefer being topside so they can see where they're going. Some prefer to fly higher than a half-inch above the surface, too.

Air Transport

The helicopter will be largely supplanted by the VTOL, or vertical takeoff and landing craft. Capable of leaping into the blue from backyards and rooftops, and setting back down in just as limited a space, these winged aircraft will be used for business and pleasure, particularly in areas away from the cities and the freeways. Faster than hovercraft, they will fly higher too; a feature that the adventurous enjoy. Speaking of adventure and sport, there will be other modes of transportation to make life exciting. The rocket belt developed after World War II will have been perfected, and some diehards will fly to work in this manner, although the law requires a quick-opening parachute for safety. Despite safeguards such as the one that prevents the firing of a rocket with less than five minutes' fuel remaining, and other warnings against power failure, an occasional rocketeer will find himself high over the city and "out of blast," a situation embarrassing not only for him but for luckless pedestrains below as well!

Sailplanes will continue to provide great sport for

those who like to copy the birds, and in 2001 there may be soaring craft whose wings are covered with light-weight panels of solar cells to drive a small electric motor and propeller for emergency use when lifting winds or currents give out.

While cross-country travel in eight hours is fast enough for many people, those in a hurry can beat that time considerably. VTOLs will provide 500-miles-an-hour speed on short runs; SSTs will make cross-country and coastal runs five times that fast. For travel to Europe and the rest of the world, the new HSTs, or hypersonic transports, burn up the sky at Mach 8 (5000 m.p.h.) and faster. Anywhere in the world in three hours will be the boast; around the world in six. The latter will be a fun trip the twenty-first-century jet set often make—flight several times faster than the sun at an altitude of twenty miles—up where the sky is really space and black as night. Lunch in Bombay, and back to SanSan by midafternoon.

For a real thrill, however, let's take a trip into space. Departing from SanSan not far from Disneyland, where simulated rocket flight thrilled youngsters not too long ago, we will ride a big space bus into orbit and race around earth several times with a spectacular sunrise and sunset each time. From hundreds of miles up we will see earth for the green and brown and blue ball it is, swathed in the cotton-batting cloud systems that are a meteorologist's dream. Then we dock at the space station that is the base for moon-bound trips. Hanging over the United States and watching sunlight sweep across the continent, we will be traveling thousands of miles an hour. After a splendid meal in the low artificial gravity of the slowly rotating station, we will board the Lunar Rocket and blast off for our natural satellite. Although we seem suspended in space, we travel at twenty-five thousand miles an hour as we escape earth's gravity, a speed that makes the HST seem slow. A three-day journey to the moon, a few days on the cold and airless ball, and the return trip. It seems like a dream, and it was until 1970, when the first men landed on the moon.

Getting three men to the moon was a multibillion-dollar effort involving the entire nation. At that time few thought the day would come when tourists, tired of Europe, Africa and the polar regions, would board rockets bound for deep space. But in 2001 tourism will be big business on the moon.

Tomorrow's Freight

Lunar ore will be "shipped" to earth simply by firing it from a long track and allowing it to fall into earth's gravity. Careful planning will insure that it lands in a safe area where the ore is then trucked out in a more conventional manner. This exotic method of transporting freight makes truck and train shipping seem old-fashioned. However, we will have new methods of getting things from here to there on earth as well. Rocket freight is an example.

Communication will be handled electronically. Instead of posting letters airmail, we'll send them with the speed of light. But some mail shipments can't be translated into electrons (although there are optimists working on that project!) even though we would like to get them to their destination faster than the HST can do the job. The best we can do is the rocket. Anywhere in the world in less than an hour is the schedule, delivered under a parachute and in shockproof containers. There will be talk of shooting *people* to their destinations too.

For terrestrial freight that is not so rush there will be methods like the great plastic "sausages" experimented with for decades. Towed by tugs or submarines, these giant carriers will hold everything from freight to fresh water. An even cheaper method of transport will let such plastic "barges" simply drift in the prevailing ocean current. Monitored by radar and occasionally nudged by a hovercraft if necessary, they will make deliveries with no fuel costs at all.

A similar freight system will be used in the air, with plastic balloons rather than marine sausages. Providing faster service than rafts that drift a few miles an hour with ocean currents, these balloons will ride the air currents, including the jet stream, at high altitude. Equipped with radar tracking equipment, parachutes and remote controls for valving operations, the balloons will be carefully monitored by ground controllers to prevent danger to air traffic or to people on earth. While pinpoint delivery is not guaranteed, most balloons will be lowered gently to earth at least somewhere near their destination and finish the trip by more conventional means.

Ocean Travel

Ocean liners that have escaped the wrecker's ball in 2001 will serve as floating classrooms, hotels and storehouses. Fast aircraft killed off the once mighty *Normandie, Queen Mary,* and others. Not enough travelers had time, money and stomachs strong enough for three days of crossing. But many will tolerate one day across the Atlantic, or two to reach Asia from SanSan. They will travel by air, a few feet above the waves, aboard highspeed hovercraft that formerly negotiated only shorter passages like that across the English Channel and a few lakes and other waterways.

Ocean-going hovercraft will be slower than an airplane but safer and less expensive. Not as economical per ton of load carried as a ship, it will be faster and thus cost less for the crossing. Freight will go by hovercraft too, when it is a shipment not feasible to send by the slower barge or submarine route.

The Moving Sidewalk

Ancient Rome in Caesar's time found it necessary to restrict the use of wheeled vehicles within the city because of congestion. In 2001 we will have gone full circle to the point where it is again necessary to shut the gates of the inner city to automobiles.

Even without wheels, however, it is possible to travel widely without wearing out any shoe leather. No one wants to walk long distances when he is used to riding. Like the cowboy who mounted up to ride across the street to the drugstore, city dwellers will demand— and get—a free ride. The solution is the moving sidewalk. First only at busy malls, but gradually reaching out from the city centers, the moving sidewalk will eliminate the onerous chore of walking. We will level off the escalator. The saying will no longer be that certain cities roll up the sidewalk at an early hour but that they stop rolling them. The more hardy humans will insist on standing as they ride, but most shoppers or other walkers will enjoy sitting on the benches that are provided.

It has been suggested that animals may regain their popularity as transport in the future. Not the horse, necessarily, but some species scientifically produced and having great intelligence. However, since it was primarily the shortage of space that eased out our four-legged friends in the first place, and since space will be in even shorter supply, it does not seem probable that we will see many animals for riding in 2001.

Even as now, we will be a nation on the go in the future, and transportation will be a large and vital part of our civilization. Despite the miracles wrought by engineers, however, there will still be traffic problems, particularly on the ground. As one expert put it recently in discussing the increase in personal vehicles, anyone who wants to get across the street had better do it now, or he might not ever make it!

5 Communication

In 1901 Guglielmo Marconi beamed the strange new radio waves across the Atlantic. Not since that time has an advance been made in the speed of message-sending; for electromagnetic waves, including radio waves, travel with the speed of light as their limit. This is rather fast and for most purposes causes no appreciable delay. However, in 2001 there will be the wish for a faster method, what with space travelers reaching out millions of miles into the galaxy and beaming hopeful queries toward intelligent beings capable of receiving and answering them. But if wishes were horses, beggars would ride, and wishing will not make electronic communication any faster in 2001. There will be a great deal more of it, nevertheless.

Benjamin Franklin stumbled onto an amazing discovery about storms. They moved with the wind along a generally fixed path from southwest to northeast, and so if one hit Philadelphia now it was bound to hit New York in about three hours. At last there was a workable storm-warning system, except for one thing: The storm moved along at thirty miles an hour or so and there was no way to get the word to the helpless victims of approaching bad weather until after the storm itself knocked them flat! Communication, even as recently as 1844, was terribly slow.

In Franklin's time a dispatch rider carried the news at the plodding speed of less than twenty miles an hour. With semaphore signals from hill to hill, or maybe a signal mirror, messages could do somewhat better. But not until Samuel Finley Breese Morse and his telegraph did communication break the time barrier. Overnight it was possible to send messages down a shiny wire at fantastic speed.

Ben Franklin was powerless to send word ahead that the storm was coming. He had only the vaguest idea of the shape and extent of the storm, even as it hammered at his home town. In 2001 we will customarily flip on television at home and see world weather as photographed by a satellite hanging a thousand miles or more out in space. So will the meteorologist. Instead of laboriously pasting together tiny scraps of information sent him from all parts of the globe to create a crude, inaccurate and dated picture of what was happening in the atmosphere, he will see it at a glance. He will also be able to spell out in accurate detail the specifics of temperature, pressure and precipitation for any area.

The weather is not the only global happening we will see as it occurs. In the 1960s communication satellites were already relaying sight and sound around the world with the speed of light. In 2001 such service will be continuously available to nearly everyone. When we phone someone—anywhere—we will see him in living color and three dimensions, just as we receive our TV programs. The miracle of "holography" will do the trick. On the life-size screens in most living rooms the result, to those of our time, would be spectacular if not unbelievable. The same thing will be true of books and magazines and newspapers. Holographs are special pictures that contain "phase information" of reflected light and thus create real images instead of flat pictures. Move your head to one side and you can see behind that tree in the foreground of a photograph. Drawings too will show depth and a wealth of detail previously unavailable; a blessing to architects, engineers and artists.

In the library of 2001 computer printouts will be made from material stored in memory devices across the country or around the world. The same service will be available at home. Our newspaper will be printed in this manner, from an attachment in the TV set. This technique will have a revolutionary effect on the book publishing world as well, in that fewer books will be printed by the publisher. For a small charge we can have them printed out right at home. Why travel to a bookstore or wait days for mail delivery? Why burden the mailman (by the way, what has happened to that gentlemen in 2001?) with all that bulk, and why print more copies than will be sold? The paper our home printer uses will be water-soluble, by the way, like many of the articles we use around the house. This makes it easily disposable, with no need for an incinerator that would smog up the neighborhood, or a trashman whose truck would do the same thing.

In 2001 you will call anyone, anywhere in the world, direct—if you can afford it. The operator won't ask your number, because there won't be an operator, and because your "voiceprint" is all the identification the computer needs. However, if your transoceanic conference call is cut off in the middle with a polite warning, it may be that you have exhausted your bank account and the phone company doesn't intend for you to be in its debt! Fantastic? No. Everything will be tied together in a global communications network. The Internal Revenue Service switched to electronic computer methods way back in the nineteen fifties. In the half-century since then, computers will have attained capacities even their originators didn't dream possible, and programers will have evolved sophisticated programs that heighten the miracle.

How about calling someone on the moon? Here we begin to notice the lag in communication caused by the "slow" speed of light. At 186,000 miles a second, it will take the laser beam we're talking on about one and a third seconds to reach our listener. So we can't say "Hi, Joe!" and get an immediate "Great, how are you?" By 2001, phone subscribers will have learned to talk around this problem. Instead of short bursts of conversation—which mean much wasted time at a fixed charge per minute, by the way—we will talk for longer periods and skilfully let our listener know when we're about through. He begins to talk while we are still talking, and that way his answer will reach us about the time we stop! For the economy—minded person making VLD (very long distance) calls, there will be an even cleverer technique. It goes like this: You call me and begin to relay all the news, interspersing questions for me to answer. As soon as I have enough information to work with, I will begin to answer, talking while you talk. This takes time to get used to, and at first will seem impossible. But it is possible, and it crams six minutes of talk into just three minutes, with no pauses at all. We can both record the chatter for later deciphering, if needed.

It would be well to remember that there is a computer monitoring all the millions of conversations going on at any given time, alert for any indication of a subversive plot, a new idea, or someone in trouble. Carefully avoiding unwarranted invasion, the electronic eavesdropper notifies the proper authorities nearest the party concerned. Suppose someone threatens to shoot the President with a laser rifle, or to jump off the nearest ten-story apartment building? Almost before he can hang up, a man from somewhere will be at his side with handcuffs or a calm talk on the fact that suicide is still against the law, and what is his problem anyhow?

Just as there is always someone who thinks he can invent perpetual motion, diehards will be striving in 2001 to find a way to communicate faster than light.

Remember, Ben Franklin wasn't really sure that messages would one day travel faster than by a courier on a fleet horse. Morse and Marconi were both called crackpots by men almost as smart as they. And there are things that go faster than light. Or seem to.

Suppose we aim a searchlight at a mountain peak 186 miles away. Then quickly we swing the light to light up another peak that is 186 miles from us also, and is also that distance from the first peak. Light will travel from one peak to another in one thousandth of a second. Suppose we then rotate our beacon at a thousand revolutions per second—something that is conceivable if not too practical. The beam of the light will then move from Peak A to Peak B in something less than one second. In fact, it will take only one sixth of a second! Therefore we have made something travel faster than light by six times. Right? Unfortunately, no. While the light did indeed sweep 186 miles in far less time than a beam starting from Point A and proceeding directly to Point B, our light carried no information from one peak to another. Here is where the "faster than light" enthusiasts get to work. Suppose there were some way to have Point A do something to the beam as it crossed that station. Wouldn't it then carry a message to Point B? No, it wouldn't. But dreamers will keep trying! Meantime, the spacecraft 186 million miles out in space will continue to encounter a lag of two thousand seconds in message sending and receiving to the moon base or earth. And two thousand seconds is more than half an hour.

Un-Babeling the World

Communication is language; what effect will global television and other developments have on language? Although the computer will translate any language into any other so nearly simultaneously that the lag is far less than that of the moon relay, the major effect of global communications will be to make most of the world speak one language—and that language is English. Americans began this one-language push when they set out to solve all the world's problems. So many missionaries, GI Joes, and other representatives of our country have taught foreigners English (sometimes because they themselves were too lazy, proud or dull to learn the foreign language, by the way) that the trend was well set when global communication came into being. For better or for worse, English and not Esperanto will become the international language and put the Tower of Babel out of commission.

On the side of Global English is the fact that, next to Chinese, it is spoken by more people than any other. Russian, the language of the second most powerful nation is spoken by only half as many as speak English. China was not in the position of pushing its language as effectively and as widely as the United States.

The greatest importance of the adoption of one language for most of the world is not in the language itself but in the effect of such uniformity of communication on a world that formerly spoke many languages. Much world strife comes from a lack of understanding. Indeed, some theorists would lay the entire blame on this factor. With all of us speaking one tongue things will be better in many respects, with less suspicion and distrust and more knowledge of how the rest of the world thinks and acts.

With the language barrier solved there will remain only one real snag to truly harmonious international relations. This is the "time barrier," caused by the fact that when it is noon in London, England, it is not yet time to get out of bed in Phoenix, Arizona. And 8 P.M. in Moscow is 4 A.M. in Sydney, Australia. Few of us want to be called to the telephone in the wee small hours, or stay up past midnight for a TV musical coming our way from some distant land we want to know better. There are a few flexible souls who can stay up all hours, or shift their waking and sleeping to suit the demands of all manner of time schedules. But for most of us it would seem that the only answer is not to sleep. That way everybody is up together; a sort of misery-loves-company approach with the added blessing of much more time to get things done. Things like watching global TV or phoning friends in Afghanistan.

There is another aspect to be considered. We discussed travel in the last chapter. Travel will be booming in 2001, and yet how much more it might have boomed had we not succeeded with global TV in living color and three dimensions! Why go on a business trip, for example, if you can hold a conference to all intents and purposes face to face with your associates without ever leaving town? Why visit a loved one halfway around the world when he or she is as close as the switch on the TV set? Of course, if the loved one is a sweetheart or spouse there might be a good argument, but the basic principle is obvious. You can climb Everest in the comfort of your own home, explore the South Pole or Clavius on the moon, and still stay close enough to the kitchen for a snack during the commercial break. (Yes, there will still be commercials in 2001.)

There is another side to this coin too, of course. TV has not killed the book trade, nor has it wiped out spectator sports; fans still fight their way into the Rose Bowl and Madison Square Garden. Perhaps global TV will even boost travel in 2001 by those who are so intrigued by the things they see on the screen they want to go there in person.

Personal Radio

In the home it is doubtful if the radio will be very popular as a separate piece of equipment. Generally it will be combined with the television entertainment center. Most radios will be portable in nature and far smaller than the miniature sets of today.

After 2001-brand TV and the videophone, will anyone waste his ears listening to radio? Yes, because it will serve a purpose. The popularity of World War II "walkie-talkies" long after the war was over showed the need for personalized communication of this sort. Many professionals and technicians began to carry pocket "pagers," whose beep beep shrilled at all hours and in all places to call the wearer. There will be tiny personal radios in 2001, usable not only for entertainment but for message-receiving and sending as well.

It will be possible to have a tiny radio implanted in the head. Pets and animals might be so equipped. Even medical patients could profit from such a technique, with their radios beaming data to the hospital or clinic charged with maintaining a watch on their health. But most small radios will clip on the ear like hearing aids or be worn on the wrist à la Dick Tracy.

Telepathy

The idea of telepathy, extrasensory perception, or, as it has more recently been called, biological radio, may flower by 2001. Living organisms, including the human body, produce electricity, and such suggestions as that of using biopower to power artificial organs is no novelty. The brain produces electricity in the radio range, and has demonstrated that it can receive and react to radio waves too. In 2001 some may communicate in this manner, relying on it for the privacy.

We convert our thoughts into spoken or written words by means of transducers, changing electrochemical impulses to sound waves or mechanical movements. And we convert sights and sounds and pressures into thoughts in our brains too. In principle there is nothing difficult about beaming thoughts in the form of electrical waves in the radio range directly to another who is "tuned" to our wavelength.

Perhaps we will enhance ESP with drugs to strengthen the generation of waves, or wear an amplifying device—not necessarily a cumbersome helmet or a surgical implant but an instrument simply built into eyeglasses or hearing aid. This amplifier with its tiny powerpack would strengthen the feeble waves in our brains and beam them out. A recipient would similarly be equipped to amplify the received waves and route them directly to his brain.

The key to whether or not we shall be communicating on this most personal basis is the need for such a system, not whether it is technically possible. The fact has been demonstrated for a long time. Examples: An Air Force scientist operated a lamp by varying his alpha rhythm. Subjects demonstrated ability to "hear" radar waves. And doctors have recorded radiation of radio waves from brain tissue—noting, by the way, that it is particularly strong in the sick or mentally disturbed.

Our present civilization has come a long way from the grunts that served as communication for the caveman. Man the talker will still be at it in 2001, his built-in urge aided and abetted by a host of new technologies that will succeed in getting the word—or rather the billions of words that are our output—to the whole wide world. And the world should be better for having heard.

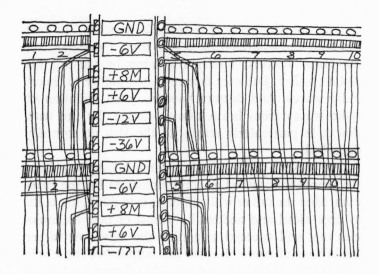

6 Computers

Like the man who couldn't see the trees for the woods,
we won't see the computers of 2001 because they will
be everywhere. We've already come across many of
them in other chapters, but they seldom look like computers. The TV set, for instance, and the telephone.
And the typewriter in the den of the average home
that's really not a typewriter but an input to a computer a dozen, a hundred, or a thousand miles away.

In the early 1960s the computer accounted for only a few billion dollars in annual business. In 2001 the computer will be the largest of all businesses and will literally run our lives.

These computers of the future will not be "high-speed morons." They will reason logically and think creatively; some may actually exceed in intelligence the humans who build them. Just as the locomotive exceeds the physical strength of its driver, so the computer will be capable of mental feats impossible to man. Machines of the industrial revolution mastered the physical world; the electronic computer will reign supreme in the mental world. And because it controls the machines, it will represent an even greater revolution in society. Computers will be the most important factor in our material lives.

Who will use computers? Government, business, education, communication, the legal profession, science, libraries, entertainment, medicine, transportation, agriculture; in fact, everyone will use computers. The Federal government will remain the largest single purchaser of computer services and use them for everything from weather prediction and control to income taxing, international relations, voting, districting, administrative functions such as payroll, promotions, purchasing, accounting, and projections of future needs.

City, state and local governments will be the next largest users of computers, and their uses parallel those of Uncle Sam. Private businesses are next, and there will be few of them that do not use the computer, no matter what the operation or how small it is. The shopping center of 2001, for example, could not function the way it will without computers, nor could the restaurant. Movies, piped in over coaxial cables, will be booked, transmitted, billed and rated for popularity by computers. Banking, which pioneered business computers, will continue to lead in developing new "software" or programing for better operations. Competitive manufacturing in 2001 will not be possible without computers. Computers will order material, take orders for merchandise, and ship those orders at the proper time. Computers will control the robots that make practically all our products, and will also design them and test them.

Highway construction—in fact, all engineering ventures—will make great use of computers. Let's see how computers will plan, build, and maintain our streets and highways, as well as calculating their costs and drafting tax measures to pay for them. Fed with data from the entire state on traffic volume, road conditions, weather, accidents, passenger count, freight volume, load during different hours of the day and days of the week, population increase or shift, business outlook, tourist trade, defense considerations, and many more factors, some of which would seem to us to have no bearing on the problem, the central computer constantly updates drawings it has made of needed additions to the system.

Each state and city will be tied to every other state and city, as well as to the central computers operated by the Federal government. Cost allocations will be constantly calculated for equitable charges to the subdivision that plans to build, those whose people drive on the system in question, and the Federal government, which will benefit in total.

Highway officials will constantly monitor the reports

of the computers. When they are convinced that the time is right they will present the program plus any needed legislation (drafted by the computer) to the government for passage and financing. If necessary, a vote of the people will be taken by computer feedback. Approval puts the new project into action immediately. Disapproval means that the computer's alternate solutions of traffic-handling will be used until such time as the new program is okayed. Let's assume it is approved, however, and a new bypass route is begun to link previously isolated freeways so that commuter traffic will be freed for faster trips to work and back.

Foremen in charge of the bypass area are briefed and given their work orders. Using mostly automated earthmoving equipment, they begin the cutting, filling and borrowing of earth spelled out in work sheets. Simultaneously other areas are getting their part of the project done. All of this work is monitored visually from a satellite high in the sky and coordinated by computers.

On the existing freeways, new ramps are built without inconveniencing the steady flow of traffic. Curving metal sections extend into space, while connecting links reach up from below. Cement is poured from huge machines running on steel guides located accurately by computer planning studies that produce scale blueprints for every foot of the project. As much of the work as possible is done in off-hours. When it must occur during rush time, electronic signals expedite the flow of traffic about the affected areas. On completion day the new bypass is phased in with no fanfare or ribbon cutting. That ceremony is on television and is generally just a pleasant way of letting the public know the new routes. The agonizing period of traffic jams, and businesses hurt by long and costly tearing up of streets, will be over because planning is done continuously on a "real time" basis, something impossible without total computer control.

On a visit to the National Department of Transportation we will see a huge videoscreen forming an entire wall of the reception room. On it, in color-coded lines that constantly change, are the freeways of the nation, almost to scale. The winking, ever-changing motion of the display will show the growth of the highway system even as we watch.

Push a button on one section of the wall and a blowup of your state's system will appear, giving the streets and highways in great detail. This map will even indicate traffic volume and—very infrequently— an accident signal. Complicated? Yes, it is complicated. So complicated that no man can understand it all or control it. That is why we will have computers do our thinking and planning for us.

The airlines pioneered the use of computers too, with automatic control for landing in bad weather, and with computer ticket-handling. In 2001 every airliner that takes off and lands will do so under control of a ground-based computer, backed up by another in the aircraft. The craft will be flown by computers on the ground, with course, altitude, and speed constantly changing and adjusting so that the total system works in the best possible way.

Reservations will no longer be necessary; you will simply go to the airport and board a plane for your destination. This will be possible because sophisticated computers very accurately predict that you will want to fly to New York on just this particular day and hour, that you will want roast beef instead of steak, and that you will be carrying forty-eight pounds of luggage. Computers, predicting that the winds will be a certain speed and direction at cruise altitude, will pump the correct amount of fuel into the tanks so that the maximum load may be carried with ample reserve fuel in case of emergency. Emergencies, by the way, will seldom occur, because computers simulate every possible kind of trouble that could occur and then take steps to see that these don't happen.

In 2001, no one has been to a bank for years, including the banker. There will be no banks in the old sense, although some institutions may maintain a tastefully designed meeting hall in an urban area as a gesture of good will and restrained advertising. Long ago banks developed the drive-in window for busy clients. In 2001, on the rare occasions when it is necessary for you to deal personally with the bank, a call on the phone does it. You will see and talk to an attractive young lady—unless you are female yourself, in which case the clerk will be an attractive young man. This is only because we still enjoy talking with attractive young people; a computer will be doing the real listening and problem-solving at hand. This personal contact will rarely occur, however, since the principle of the small service charge you pay is to make it unnecessary for you even to think about money!

Computers will aid doctors in 2001, too. In fact, the computer will actually be the doctor in some cases. Let's go to a clinic in the suburbs not far from where you live. A routine checkup is given even though you don't have to undress. Electronic sensors measure temperature, muscle tone, skin color, breathing, and the like. X rays and ultrasonics probe inside for trouble. A pleasant voice asks how we are and then proceeds to tell us the results of the examination. There is a congestion indicated in the chest; will we please cough and describe the sensation. Any pain? Difficulty with breathing? Another X ray is taken and the trouble is isolated. A prescription is printed out, but like the old handwritten ones the doctor provided, we can't read it. It is in computer language, to be fed into the blender at the druggist's.

"I think that should do the trick," the doctor says. "But I want you to give me a call from home tomorrow night so I can take a look at you." End of office call. The doctor is an electronic voice and the mind of the accumulated medical knowledge of the world. The entire consultation will be added to our medical file. We may consult it by TV anytime we want, and the clinic will call us periodically for checkups. There are still human doctors, of course, to oversee clinics, monitor surgical machines, do research and teach the computer even more than it already knows.

There will be psychologists and psychiatrists, although the latter will become more organically oriented. A consultation with them will likely lead to a prescription for drugs or a new diet rather than a change of occupation or a long vacation in the country.

Steps to the Super Computer

Realistic gauges of a computer's capability are its information-storage capacity, or "memory," and its speed of operation. In the latter department electronic computers quickly exceeded the human brain. Neurons operate at about a thousandth-of-a-second or "millisecond" speed. Computers advanced from milliseconds to microseconds, then to nanoseconds and picoseconds. A picosecond is a trillionth of a second! If the increase in capacity and speed of electronic computers continues at the rates achieved thus far, by 2001 they will exceed by millions of times the performance of today's models.

ENIAC, the first electronic computer, was a monster brain in size, made up of thousands of vacuum tubes and other large electronic components. Early cynics of the computer age protested that a computer with the logical capacity of a human brain would be as large as the Empire State Building and require Niagara Falls to keep it cool. In 2001 there will be computers with as many logical elements as the human brain (some ten billion), that can be carried in the palm of one hand. While the computer industry expanded tremendously in the half century since its introduction, individual computers shrank in size. This was accomplished by the miniaturization of the various elements.

The first generation of computers used electronic tubes, a handful of which matched the volume and weight of the human brain. It was pointed out that even if technology could produce the ten billion switches for a penny each, wiring them together would be such an added expense that the whole world could not afford such an electronic brain. Since this was so obviously true, computer designers went another way.

The second generation used transistors and other "solid state" switches. These tiny elements were smaller, cheaper, and more dependable than vacuum tubes, so computers likewise became smaller, cheaper and more dependable. The number of switches grew from thousands to millions in large computer complexes. This was still a long way from ten billion, of course, and until another generation of computers could be produced the argument held about high cost. The new generation was called integrated-circuitry computers.

Transistors are single elements, produced on a tiny chip or die of germanium, silicon, or other material. Integrated circuits are hundreds and even thousands of elements or electronic switches on a single die! And all of these are produced automatically, with the interconnections made on a wholesale basis instead of individually by human operators as was the case with transistors. Integrated circuits have grown to something called LSI, or large-scale integration, by our time, but not until the next generation of "grown" circuits will the component density of an electronic computer match that of the human brain.

Nature grows living things and also inorganic materials such as crystals. Computer designers will ask for and get crystals that are actually millions upon millions of tiny elements useful for computer switching.

Early computers with only a few hundred thousand switches seemed capable of mathematical and logical processes that humans couldn't match. This was so because only a relatively few of the ten billion neurons in the human computer are used effectively. Nature apparently operates on a system of redundancy, or extra parts to guarantee reliable operation. In the first grown computers only a few percent of the total elements produced will be operational. This will be no problem, for the computer will be "wired" automatically in a way that bypasses the faulty switches. However, as experience is gained and computers learn how to grow better computers, more effective elements will result. In 2001 very high yields will be expected in fourth-generation equipment.

There will be fifth-generation computers in the laboratories. These computers, in theory at least, will match the information density of the living cell, with as many elements as the cell has genes. Operating on tiny amounts of electricity, and interconnected with laser beams instead of wires, the new computers will be gradually phased into existing systems as needed.

Studies of the brain benefit the computer, and vice versa. Each results in more understanding of the other, and each advance can mean a better world. Computers help us to understand our minds, and our minds in turn help us to construct computers to improve our material life. While the last half century is generally referred to by the appealing and well-justified title of the Computer Age, in 2001 the Age of Reason will be a better description and a more accurate one. Computers do not exist for themselves, but only to help man think and plan a better world.

Computers and Human Rights

The fear that computers threaten an invasion of privacy will prove largely false. When man first began to keep records or to write diaries he opened the door for others to learn his affairs. The computer, while it is faster and has a wider field of information, can do no more in principle than older methods of record-keeping. Those fearful of the computer in 2001 must have something to hide in the first place; the computer will not be nosy or a peeping Tom. In fact, some people may be disappointed that the computer couldn't care less about some of the confidences they reveal to it! Coding will be permitted in many computer storage applications so that businesses or individuals can protect a process, invention, or business plan. By the same token, the cheat or schemer will learn that the computer is a relentless discoverer of such misdeeds. The Internal Revenue Service, for example, is called the electronic bloodhound by those who have sought unsuccessfully to defraud Uncle Sam of taxes due him. But as for simply keeping a secret that is not illegal, committing records to the computer may prove the safest way to hide information from the world. Unlike humans, the computer gets no thrill out of prying. And since human eyes seldom see computer data the job of ferreting out embarrassing information becomes even harder. In 2001, the post card writer who once feared that the mailman might read his words need no longer worry, since his message goes direct to the addressee with no one else to see it along the way.

More than any single other development, the electronic computer will shape and change the world in 2001. As the machine age multiplied our muscle power, the computer age will augment our mind power. By the turn of the century, survival without these adjuncts to our brains will be as unthinkable as it would be today to get along without mechanical things. Fortunately it seems that the computer revolution will come about much less painfully than did the industrial revolution.

7 Education

There is the story of a little boy who was asked how well he did on his first day of school. "Not so good," he said disappointedly. "I have to go back again tomorrow!" There will still be school in 2001, but there will be dramatic changes by then. Most noticeable outwardly will be the teaching technology that the computer and the teaching machine—or the synthesis of the two—will create. Classrooms will be learning laboratories, equipped with global TV, computer links with the libraries of the world, teaching teams from professions and vocations and arts, field trips that range around the world, and lectures by the great men of many endeavors.

Teaching, career planning, psychological counseling, testing, grading and scheduling will be done painlessly and automatically. Students may go to school anywhere, and at flexible hours they arrange to suit themselves. The school will reach into the home via the computer terminal and the TV screen; the homebound student will reach out in the same way to the school outside. Much technical teaching will be done by computer simulators—driving training for example, as well as flying, equipment operation, plant management, and engineering.

The school library of 2001 may have but few volumes on its shelves, but in seconds it will print whatever others a student wants. Equipped with a tape memory instead of book stacks, and tied to the memories of other libraries around the country and the world, it will print out at request any of the world's wealth of written material. It will translate from foreign languages, conduct literature searches and furnish abstracts on command. The library will be a powerful tool in the hands of one skilled in computer use, and our student in 2001 will be very skilled in that regard.

Even more important, though not as outwardly evident as the changes in educational tools, will be changes in the very concepts and philosophy of education.

Basic Education: 2001

Accustomed to an advanced, computerized technology from infancy, the preschool youngster of 2001 will learn to play with others and to express himself creatively in a variety of ways that include painting, music, and tape recordings. While some conventional symbols will be taught and certain responses asked for, care will be taken not to stifle the creativity of the young pupil with too much regimentation and formality. Psychological and aptitude tests will point toward strong and weak points in his makeup and his education will be shaped to make use of his strengths while reinforcing his weaknesses.

Early schooling, supplemented by home and cultural experiences, will not be aimed at cramming many facts into his head but will seek to instill in him a curiosity for knowledge and a pleasure in learning things for himself. Only after he has "learned how to learn" will he be taught specific things. However, experimental classes with very young children have demonstrated that they can comprehend such things as geometry and logic. In fact, some educators feel that the very young child is more receptive to such concepts than he will be after some years of conventional school work. Preschool classes at age three, or at least parental encouragement at this level, may be standard in the twenty-first century.

With a "voicewriter" the youngster will learn to spell. By 2001 such a machine will type out what is spoken to it, and another will speak what is typed on it. The child will also engage in conversations with a computer, which will not only answer questions but ask them, too. Since much of life will revolve around computers, students will begin early to work with them.

Only when a youngster is ready to move upward again from his newly reached plateau will he be encouraged to do so. Fluency in language, both verbally and in writing, will be stressed, and the "social promotion" of the earlier years of the twentieth century will not be resorted to. Thus the student will never know the embarrassment of reaching college age without knowing how to read or write.

Although the first few years of grade school will be most informal, with no obvious attempt at formalized classes, schedules or curricula, this may be the most productive part of education. It is futile to try to impart learning to someone who is not ready to receive it.

Which courses will be taught and which discarded? Surely in 2001 there will be many substitutions in catalogs. With goals for education realistically defined, and accurate testing over many years and a great number of students to find how well they achieved those goals, educators will have had time to perfect the classes that are expected to do the job. Nor will the curricula then be as rigid as in the past.

In the upper grades, classes will be somewhat more formal, but not nearly so as nowadays. Most teaching will be by TV, drawing on tapes or live instruction from a central location in the city, or from another city or country, to take the best advantage of top teachers. Again, the computer will serve as teacher and record-keeper. There will be much variety toward the top grades, although the student will be encouraged to develop his best abilities, while improving those that need work.

All youngsters will be given kindergarten and grade school education through a certain number of grades as a basis for advanced education. By the time grade school is finished, the student will have been informed of his best career possibilities through thorough counseling with both the computer and human teachers. The myth that all should strive for college or university education will have given way to the realization that for some a shorter period of technical training may be all that is desired. Why submit someone to several years of higher education he neither wants nor needs but which may hurt his pride and confidence? By the same token, why limit to four years someone who can profit from twice that much education?

Education will have a number of goals, each tailored to a certain kind of student. The very bright will be afforded every opportunity to acquire as much schooling as they can profit from. Those above average will have programs aimed toward fitting them for the profession of their choice and aptitude. Average students will have a choice of two or four-year colleges, with further education if their performance and interest justifies it. All students will have the opportunity to finish high school, with assistance if they need it, plus junior college if they desire it. Much emphasis will be given to vocational and technical training where a student's abilities indicate that kind of future.

Realizing that learning rates are different, educators will make it possible for slower students to continue their schooling as long as they require, and of course anyone will be privileged to attend night school or adult education classes.

It will be recognized in 2001 that there are different kinds of learning. Typing can be taught with a teaching machine, but the writing of successful novels cannot be taught at all—only encouraged and aided with helpful knowledge of spelling, vocabulary and grammar.

Sports may well be divorced from formal connection with school, as will many cultural programs. These will be available to the community as a whole and will thus be part of life and not just part of school.

Instead of school for nine months of the year, classrooms will be open the year round to make more economical use of facilities and also provide opportunity for the eager student. Vacations will be scheduled as the family desires, since courses and testing will be flexible because of individual instruction. Furthermore, it will be possible to make up work in a distant city with records transmitted back to the home school immediately.

Industry will educate many of its people itself. The solution will be a basic education in school, plus specialized training and retraining by business. Two years in school and two years of on-the-job training will result in a far better employee for a particular job than the whole four years in formal schoolwork.

School will be even more of a meeting place for the entire family by 2001. Already there is an increasing cultural and recreational nature in schools compared with a generation ago. Then, school taught reading, writing and arithmetic and left nearly everything else to the devices of the student and his family. Now it is obvious that there is much to be gained by more use of the physical and cultural facilities of school, particularly at the higher levels. Adult education will continue to grow, particularly with more leisure time available for learning. Music, sports and civic affairs will be much more in evidence on the campus of 2001.

There will be less importance attached to the financial status of a pupil and his geographical location. The trend has been slowly but surely away from financing at the local property-tax level. School financing will be increasingly spread out across an entire state; the Federal government seeks to equalize the dollar differences from state to state. Education will be paid for from income taxes; thus the student having received the most from his schooling will contribute the most. By 2001 there will be equality of quality education, regardless of who or where the student is.

The words "school of one's choice" will have new meaning. There will be more private schools, and tax credits or cash grants will be available to students wishing to attend them rather than public schools. Such a development will do much to strengthen the educational establishment by providing healthy competition and a variety of thinking in terms of curricula and administration.

Like everything else, education will profit much from global communication networks. On-the-spot news and informational programs from around the world will help make students aware of what is happening. With two-way communication, actual conversations with students in other parts of the world will be possible. Beyond that, there will be more actual trips to foreign lands, not only at the college level but in grade school as well. The exchange student idea will be expanded so that many students, instead of the fortunate handful now chosen, will journey abroad and live with foreign families. Perhaps it may become a formal part of the course to spend a year or more on foreign soil learning a new language and a different way of life.

Teaching Machines

Two and two will always be four; the laws of motion are the same as when Newton proposed them. Generally the truth remains the truth. But methods of getting that truth to those who need to know it change; sometimes for the better.

The first teaching was done by example. A caveman taught his son how to kill a sabertooth tiger before the latter could reverse the process. A cavewoman showed her daughter how to cook food. How do we know this was the first method of teaching? Simply because these things were taught before man had a language, written or spoken. Before any teaching can be done, there must be something to be taught.

Words helped immeasurably. Along with his example, the primitive hunter could explain why he did what he did in just such a manner. It was generally evident that the basic reason for the kill was to obtain food—and to keep from becoming food for the quarry instead. But the spoken word, the verbal lesson, embellished the teaching process. In 2001 we will still be teaching age-old truths, but we will impart them in more sophisticated ways.

It has been suggested that the first teaching machine was the hickory switch, with which a schoolmaster speeded up the learning process in his less diligent pupils. This early device is remembered in the classic advice to "spare the rod and spoil the child." While some psychologists believe that punishment results in more learning than either reward or a combination of punishment and reward, it is a poor teacher who tries to impart the contents of a text simply by beating on his charges. The theory of "reinforcement" is fine, but the ideal teaching machine imparts learning along with punishment.

There is a teaching machine called the Basically Oriented Organizer of Knowledge, more familiarly known as a BOOK. This modest device, which began as marks scratched in the sand with a pointed stick and progressed through the papyrus scroll to today's computer-edited and printed volume, will most likely continue to be the mainstay of education. Despite the threat of television, the printed word will remain the root of knowledge. And since someone has to write such words, the human teacher will still be around in 2001. He or she will have a great deal of help in the task, however.

The first tools in the recent wave of teaching-machine technology were "programed" textbooks. Such books presented a certain amount of information and then asked questions of the reader. A successful answer advanced him to the next block of information; failure to answer correctly necessitated a rereading of the material or perhaps a new approach to the same information, followed again by another question until success was attained. The obvious advantage—and the possible disadvantage—of such an approach is that it does not require a human teacher and allows the student to proceed as rapidly or as slowly as his abilities permit. All books are teaching machines, or should be, but the programed book is specially designed to make use of psychological techniques or reinforcement and step learning.

Audio recording is another teaching device that eliminates the need for a human teacher on the scene. Today we have campus "labs" in which students listen to tapes in the solitude of a carrel, or booth. While some teachers rooted in conventional techniques bemoan the absence of old Socrates the master teacher, learning alone can work, although for best results it is supplemented with personal contact from time to time.

During World War II it was demonstrated that teaching machines, from the programed text to film strips, movies and mechanical devices, could impart knowledge faster and more thoroughly than usual methods. This was generally used in the case of technical training, but language can be taught in similar fashion, as can mathematics, history and other subjects. With the coming of the electronic computer the teaching machine had a powerful new helper.

The teaching machine exploded like the atom bomb and at the same time, and for a while it seemed that there would be a beneficial fallout from the new weapon. However, despite many good results, the technique has not been widely adopted and today only a few schools are using it profitably. The machine's proponents, while admitting the setbacks of the last decade or so, feel that technology will advance rapidly in the years ahead so that by 2001 the teaching machine will achieve its great promise and be a potent instrument in the hands of the teacher. In 2001 the electronic teaching machine will be flexible enough to handle a single student or a classroomful all at once. It will ask questions, weigh answers and vary its teaching approach to match the knowledge and learning rate of the student. Nevertheless it should not take the place of the human teacher any more than books have done down through the ages.

There are those who fear the teaching machine. Some see the "learning box" as a device capable of brainwashing a student into believing whatever the "teacher" programs the box to teach. Dr. B. F. Skinner, the well-known psychologist and inventor of the "conditioning" apparatus called the Skinner Box, once taught pigeons to play Ping-Pong and even to guide bombs through the air. Surely a Skinner Box can teach humans to do a lot more than play Ping-Pong and guide bombs.

Thus far we have stayed on safe ground in predicting the education of the future. Now let's try some of the more imaginative possibilities that have been suggested. It may be that revolutionary breakthroughs will affect the educational process so that the school of 2001 will be something we hardly recognize.

Speed reading has long been resorted to for accelerating learning. Although there is much controversy as to whether one can read comprehensively at several thousand words a minute (or only be aware of what color ink was used in the printing and whether or not the illustrations are in color), it is obviously worth while to be able to read rapidly. What of oral learning? A technique called speech compression now under experimentation may result in transmission of speech at speeds double normal. A tape recording listened to at three hundred words or more a minute instead of at the normal speed produces a squeaky, Donald Duck gabble that is difficult if not impossible to understand. The speech-compression technique involves changing the frequency in speeding up the record, so that it sounds faster but is still intelligible.

Another process for imparting knowledge in a different way is called sleep teaching. A commercial firm markets records to be played under one's pillow. The information is supposed to be taken in by the brain unconsciously and to be available later when the learner desires to recall it. The system is controversial and about on a par with the so-called subliminal advertising stunt, in which advertising messages flashed on the screen so briefly that they are not consciously seen are nevertheless registered on the unconscious mind. Later, the subliminally reached customer runs out to buy a bag of Subliminal Potato Chips or a Subliminal Roadster without really knowing why he does it. Perhaps even this weird technique might be adapted to education, although it would seem more suited to purposes of propaganda or subversion.

The Transfer of Learning

The most exciting educational prospect of all is the possibility of transferring learning from one mind to another directly, without any intermediate steps like speaking, writing or demonstrating. Called memory transfer, this consists of taking an extract from the brain of a trained animal and feeding it or injecting it into an untrained one.

Pouring knowledge through a funnel into a student's head has long been the dream of some teachers—and perhaps a few frustrated students as well. Some scientists claim to have done just that, in effect. In early experiments planaria, or flatworms, were taught a certain response to a stimulus such as a flash of light. When these educated worms were then ground up and fed to uneducated planaria, lo and behold, the recipients had acquired the learning!

This smart-pill approach suggests the idea of grinding up old college profs and feeding them to the undergrads, and many scientists say that learning transfer makes about that much sense. Nevertheless, other scientists stoutly maintain that they have taught by transferring some substance that seems to affect the brain. Included in the animals so "taught," in addition to the flatworm, are rats, mice and hamsters. More recently, mice have been taught fear by being fed an extract taken from mice who learned the fear through experience. And in the eyes of some psychologists, if one bit of learning can be imparted, the theory is proved. If a student can learn a single response, he can theoretically learn the sum of all knowledge if it is properly bottled and injected into him!

Short of learning transfer, there is the idea of treating a brain chemically to make it learn faster. This idea is more palatable to conventionalists, and some positive results have been claimed. The drug Cylert was marketed after scientists who tried it on human patients said it seemed to indicate some memory improvement in elderly patients. But more scientists pooh-poohed the whole notion.

Much of a nation's wealth is in its knowledge. There will be much more to know in 2001, and we will call on new and sophisticated techniques to impart this knowledge to a much greater percentage of the world's population. As we succeed in feeding the world we must also work toward nourishing the minds of all.

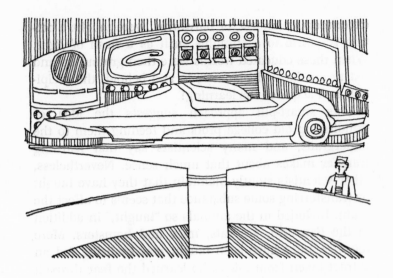

8 Vocation

In 2001 you'll work less and enjoy it more. You will be more skilled, whether you are a professional or vocationally trained, and you will spend part of each year keeping up with new developments in your particular endeavor. Your salary will be several times that paid now for comparable work, but you may never receive a paycheck. The chances are good that you will have something to do with computers, and that you will spend part of your working years abroad.

You will live some distance from work in 2001 but reach your office or plant quickly because of efficient traffic handling on the freeways. Whether you are professionally or technically trained, you will have received the last two years or so of your training on the job, or at least under the supervision of the firm you work for. With vocational counseling and effective aptitude testing you will be better fitted into a career, To make work even more interesting, your wider training, plus the general integration of business into a more unified system, will make it possible for you to choose among more possibilities. Or to change your work from time to time to keep from going stale.

By 2001, automation—and computerized automation or "cybernation"—will have been putting people out of work for half a century. Strangely, however, it will be difficult to find enough people to get all the work done! The computer itself is a prime example. It can put a dozen men or a hundred men out of work; yet next year there will be more men working than ever before. This is not just because it takes men to build, maintain and operate computers but because computers open up new lines of work. They make it possible to do many more things that are desirable but were not possible in the old days with old methods.

In times past it was almost unheard of for mothers to have jobs. Today most of them do, and if they all suddenly left work there would be the worst shortage of help in history. Even with most families holding two jobs, the unemployment rate is about as low as it ever was. So it seems that automation and computers are not wiping out jobs but creating them faster than we can produce people to fill them. In 2001 there will most likely be jobs for all who desire them. Those who do not, for one reason or another, will most likely be guaranteed an annual "wage" anyhow.

With all the work that must be done we will still be able to work less time. In 1900 the average American worker labored for about fifty-three hours a week to provide himself and his family with a living. Today the work week is much shorter, with forty hours pretty much the standard. This trend toward less working hours continues; in some fields the 35-hour week is already standard. By 2001 the average jobholder will probably work about thirty hours. This means only four days a week, with three days off to be used for other purposes. Besides this, it is almost certain that vacations will be longer, with perhaps a month as the average instead of the present two weeks.

How can we work less and have more? The answer is the improved productivity of new technology. In the old days when it took a cobbler a couple of days to fashion a pair of boots, the purchaser had to labor about that long to buy those boots if the cobbler was to earn a good living. Today, with automated equipment, better shoes require less production time, and it is seldom that we spend two days' wages for a pair of shoes unless they are indeed something special. The same thing is true for automobiles, beefsteak and books. What were once luxuries—books, for example, because the type was hand-set and the press hand-operated— today are available to most of the population at reasonable prices. In 2001, thirty hours of work will produce more goods or services than forty do now.

By 2001 retirement may also come as much as ten years earlier. Again, the reason is technology. It will take fewer people to produce what the population as a whole needs for the good life. Earlier retirement is certainly a blessing to look forward to. In the days when your parents' parents were working and raising families, it was not unheard of for men to labor all their lives. Retirement just never came for some hard-working individuals. Even horses fared better and were often turned out to pasture after a reasonable time behind the plow or wagon—even sooner from the race-track!

In 2001 the working man can look forward to a work-year of about 1,800 hours, or some two hundred less hours than in 1968. Retirement age for Social Security pensions may have dropped to fifty-five years instead of sixty-five, and many will be able to retire at fifty or even younger. Man will be spending less than half his years in working, and during those working years he will actually labor less than twenty-five percent of the time. With hours like that it is hard to imagine complaining of overwork—but we probably will!

Despite advancing technology and society, the four basic occupation categories will remain. First there will be those who provide the raw materials for our needs, the hunters, fishermen, farmers and miners. Hunters will be less important in a world that increasingly produces food by methods that approach those of automated industry. Fishermen may be increasingly important, however, for reasons we will see in a later chapter. The farmer will still have the job of feeding most of us. The miner will not only provide minerals for power production and metalworking but may even begin to feed some of us!

Workers in the second category are the processors, who convert timber to useful wood products, grain into bread, ore into sheets of metal, steers into T-bone steaks. Third come the service industries that are needed by the first two groups, including repairmen and delivery drivers. In the fourth are those who perform services for everyone, such as doctors, lawyers and government workers.

For those who have grown up in the vocational and professional system of 2001 it will seem quite natural and understandable, but specific jobs, businesses, and industries would seem mighty sophisticated from today's viewpoint.

Today the computer "cybernates" factories and railroads, blends gasoline and ice cream, saws timber with least waste, and processes checks more quickly and more accurately than a battery of yesterday's bank tellers. In 2001 however, the computer will be as ubiquitous in business and industry as copying machines and intercoms are today.

Not too long ago we paid our bills and made purchases with cash. Paper money and coins were the life blood of business. "In God we trust; all others pay cash" was a motto only half in jest in many places of business. But the checkbook superseded the bulging or thin wallet, and the credit card is fast taking the place of the billions of checks we write annually. By 2001 money will be a joked-about relic of inefficient days of yore—as needless as the weighty strings of shells natives once used for legal tender, or as the blocks of salt, and even animals, once exchanged in kind in the marketplace.

How It Will Work

To get an idea how the new system will work, let's take a look at a business transaction you'll accomplish in 2001. You visit a travel agent and decide to take a trip to the South Pole, since your hobby is riding motorized sleds across the ice. The cost is X dollars, so the agent places your card in the machine to register payment. In miscoseconds a central computer a thousand miles away records the transaction. You forgot to check your balance at home before you left, and jokingly tell the agent you hope the machine doesn't light up and say "Tilt!" If you are short of funds the computer won't handle the situation this bluntly, of course. Instalment payments will be arranged automatically and billed against your future salary. Unless your employment record is poor, that is.

In case you had not been able to come into the travel agency in person you could have phoned, and your picture on the screen would have been scanned for identification. Or your voiceprint would have been sufficient. Stored away on tape, or in some other kind of memory bank, are your financial records, updated constantly as wages accrue to your account, with taxes automatically deducted, along with payments for goods and such services as your vacation trip, retirement credit, donations to charity, insurance and investments.

Let's look at a couple of specific jobs and see how they will be taken care of in 2001. Merchandising, for example. You are the manager of a hardware store, and this Monday morning you and two assistants are checking for the week's business. An airfreight delivery of items was brought to the service door a few minutes before you arrived at work, so you unpack these and place them on the proper shelves. Then you spend a few minutes with a new girl who will handle the video shopping department. You show her how to operate the merchandise selector switches that display various products for a caller on one of the many UHF channels available. Everything is in order. Promptly at 9 A.M. the front door unlocks automatically and the day begins. Vacation time is coming and business is brisk, but everything goes smoothly. Shoppers stroll about the store, selecting needed items by marking cards with the appropriate punches. When they have completed their purchases they insert the card at what was once called the cashier's station or check stand. Automatically the purchases are brought in on a conveyor belt from the supply room out back as the cost is figured and billed against the purchaser's account. If desired, the items are delivered to his home.

In addition to those shopping personally, others are calling from home or work to make selections for delivery or later pickup. Remote TV cameras flash pictures and descriptions of various items, with special help from the new employee you have just briefed.

Perhaps you work in a production plant. Let's take a look at the job of technician, auto-body assembly, in the electric car division in 2001. The assembly line is vaguely like that of today. There is no chassis of steel members to serve as a backbone of the finished car. Instead, subassemblies of motorized wheels and body sections come together at Station A. Your job is to make sure that the robot assemblers function properly throughout the shift. Normally this is no problem, since they are programed to do each step at exactly the right time and in exactly the right way. Once in a great while mistakes happen, however, like the time four fenders on one car were each a different color! Your boss still has that classic rainbow model on display in the training center as an example of the famous old "Murphy's Law"—Whatever can happen will. This morning all goes well, with blue fenders mated to blue bodies and all motors operating properly in the wheel-test section before final inspection. You and your four assistants, aided by a dozen remote TV screens, keep production at a hundred per cent for the shift, pleased with the knowledge that several hundred more com-muter model electrics will be shipped tonight for de-livery in the region your branch plant supplies.

Global Business

The age-old goal of one world is somewhat closer in 2001, and to a large extent because of global trade. With high-speed transportation of men and equipment, and instantaneous communication between all parts of the world, global business is a reality. As a result, the chances for travel are good for the man or woman who wants to see and be a part of the world and not just his corner of it. You work in a bank in the United States this year, or this month. Next year or next month you spend some time in Sydney, Australia, or in Calcutta, India, or in Durban, South Africa, while men and women from those places take your job here at home. Maybe you like life better there, or in Ireland, or Spain, or Argentina. So you live there for as long as you like. Or you can keep moving around until you find a spot you think ideal—or just because you like moving around! If one world is to come, this is probably the way it will come—with the working together of all nationalities in a common interest of business for the good of the world.

It seems wise to let those who do a thing best, cheapest or safest do it. Why should a nation build steel mills if it will cost several times as much for them to produce steel as those of another nation? Especially when Nation B can produce fabrics and certain agricultural items far more successfully and more cheaply than steelmaker Nation A? Certainly overspecialization can be stultifying, and this is not always the best way to manage. But there is a wise and rewarding compromise somewhere in between. By 2001 we should have moved decisively in this direction in world trade, safeguarding national security and best interests, of course.

The Dollar

While we have said we shall have little need for dollars as such in 2001, it is interesting to discuss money as a kind of yardstick of material progress. In 1965 the GNP or Gross National Product in the United States was almost $700 billion. For each of our nearly two hundred million citizens we produced something more than $3,500, then. This is on the average, of course. Some of us got far less than $3,500, and some got far more. What will be the GNP in 2001? Some estimates place it as high as seven times that of 1965—in other words, about $5,000 billion, or $5 trillion. For those of us not yet accustomed to even millions, the jump from billions to trillions is breathtaking. A trillion dollars is a fantastic amount of money. You would have to spend $150 million per *second* to get rid of the $5 trillion as fast as it will be produced, a prodigal undertaking that would tax the ingenuity of all but the bureaucratic spender.

Because the population will increase too, to three hundred million or more, the per capita income will not be seven times as high as that we now enjoy. But it will still be a nice $12,000 per person, or $48,000 for a family of four! The fly in the ointment is something called inflation. The cost of living will increase several fold by 2001. Statistics can be interpreted in as many ways as there are statisticians, of course. The pessimist tends to claim that inflation wipes out any possible gain. For example, although today the average income is much higher than it was in the 1930s the dollar is now worth only a fraction of its old worth. Does this mean that we are no better off now than before? Obviously this is not true, for our standard of living is much higher than it was in the 1930s.

It is also not true that jobs for the unskilled are vanishing. In 2001 there will still be work for the nonprofessional, for instance in yard work, in small restaurants, in garbage collection, and in small farming and other manual labor.

To maintain a high standard of living for all we must have highly mechanized and sophisticated industry and agriculture but it will be possible to live "outside" this system at a very unsophisticated level. It may be that as men have more leisure time some of them will revert to "cottage" industry and primitive farming methods as a way of life they prefer. For example, while the average income in 2001 may be $12,000 per person and it will require just about all of that to live in the style we shall have become accustomed to (several automobiles, an elegant home, fine clothes, much travel and many services), life will be possible—and maybe even more desirable—with far less expenditure of money. This will be so particularly as new areas are opened up with cheap power and water. Many that are now desert could "bloom as the rose" with irrigation and offer a way of life many retired people—and some not yet retired—might enjoy.

Every man, then, will not be a Ph.D. In fact, it is quite probable that the technician—the service man—will have achieved a new stature and his job will be more sought after as people realize that we need not be intellectuals to make a good living and enjoy the good life.

9 And Vacation

In 2001 you will spend one third more of your life pursuing a hobby or indulging in recreation. What will you do with this additional leisure time? Indeed, the idea suggested in the chapter on communication—that of sleeping less—would result in even more time for leisure!

Television will be with us, the bulk of it still given to

light entertainment paid for by advertisers. For some, television will be the means of filling the hours left over. Live theater will enjoy one of its periodic revivals, and even in small cities there will be fairly frequent performances. Plays will be evenly divided between those of writers of earlier times, such as O'Neill, Saroyan, Williams and Albee, and the newer crop of playwrights. However, improvising from a standard plot will be popular, too.

Sports will still be popular, with national baseball played in more than a score of huge arenas covered with plastic and safe against inclement weather. Football will have moved inside too, with soccer, polo and most of the sports once played in the open. This will be partly a carryover from the days when outside smog was so bad that one couldn't see the winning home run or touchdown pass! The attendance at such events will hold up well in spite of the improvement in television. Most major sporting events will be professional in 2001, since the change in educational philosophy. School sports were professional in every sense of the word and little was lost in divorcing them from school campuses. Golf will be enjoyed by many, although some old-timers will complain that riding an aircar about a well-manicured layout and hitting the ball without rising from one's seat is not the game at all.

Track records will be interesting in comparison with those of a generation ago. The three-and-a-half-minute mile will have been run a number of times, with "augmented breathing" a legal technique on the track. The hundred-yard-dash mark will be under nine seconds too. Pole vaulters will have cleared twenty-two feet, at high altitude to take advantage of the lowered air resistance and gravity. Augmented breathing, "supercharges" the athlete to make up for the thinner air.

In 2000 the Olympics, which continue to be held every four years, may well be staged in Lunar City. Since all records will be broken in altitude events, a complicated adjustment of measurements is being worked out by computer to make them comparable to earlier marks. Athletes must report to the moon six months ahead of the games to acclimate themselves to the low gravity and atmospheric pressure of the satellite, as well as to learn the very different techniques for running, jumping and throwing.

The greatest changes in recreation will be most noticeable in the air and in the water. Skydiving began many decades ago, but now jumpers will wear small plastic wings instead of 'chutes. Cavorting in the sky like human aircraft, the new breed will do aerobatics, cross-country flying, speed dashes and spot landings. This will be the most thrilling sport on earth, although some moon sports will challenge it.

Skindiving will persist, with many new variations. The advent of tiny nuclear-powered jet drives will add speed and distance to the diver's bag of tricks. New "gills" will permit breathing of water, so that enthusiasts can spend an entire vacation beneath the surface of the sea, traveling hundreds of miles and often out-swimming fish.

Surfing will be popular, but with new jet-propelled boards that give ten times the thrill of the old-fashioned technique of simply going downhill on a wave. The new surfer will fly over the water, controlling the board with foot switches and achieving speeds up to fifty miles an hour.

Free ballooning will be popular again, after a long

lull. One innovation will be a gas balloon that can reach very high altitudes and remain in the air for several days on one filling of its low-cost gas. Deflated, balloon and harness can be carried by one man, and the sport will be combined with hiking into rough country, from which the balloon ascension is made back to the starting point.

Sports innovations will constantly be available for young and old folks alike. On the "Big Blast," a high-speed wind blown straight up into the air by large fans, customers will "fly" to great altitudes, up to a hundred feet, and then drop back to the ground in perfect safety. Another thrill ride might be the "Tether-Whirl," in which riders will be fitted with wings like those of skydivers and with a tow hook that whirls them fast enough to make the wings effective for limited aerobatics while whirling about a central column.

The success of Disneyland will lead to many more such acres of entertainment. In 2001 we will find the original Disneyland ten times its original size and at least one similar institution in each of the other states. They, like the original, will be packed with more adults than children, proving that we never outgrow the need for play. At these havens for leisure the key is entertainment. Not sport, either spectator or participant, but pure entertainment. Some of it will have the added value of informational content, like models of "Lunar City" in several of the fun cities we visit. But by and large we will go there and return again and again simply to be entertained, to forget our cares and quite literally to become as children again.

The subject of vacations is fascinating to speculate on. Not too long ago it was commonplace to spend as much as half of a two-week vacation going and coming from the seashore or mountain resort we had selected. In fact, many people chose to remain in town rather than waste the time traveling on jammed highways where finding accommodation for overnight stops was more effort than the pleasure of the trips. The airplane changed that, and even now many vacationers spend almost all of their free time thousands of miles from home.

By 2001 it will be standard procedure to jet halfway around the world for a couple of days of leisure in some exciting place.

Travel will be very popular, and many will spend their leisure time and money in this form of recreation. The reasons are many, one being that most adults in 2001 will have spent a year or more living and working with people in another part of the world. As a result they have friends around the world and relatives scattered from Australia to the Antarctic. Traveling cheaply halfway around the world in two hours, a computer-programmer whose real love is surfing can spend a three-day weekend riding the big ones in Hawaii, Australia, South Africa and Peru; a teacher who loves music can jet to Rome, Austria and Moscow for concerts a day apart and be back before her class fresh and alert Monday morning. And how about a vacation on the moon in 2001?

Much leisure time will be spent exploring our natural satellite a quarter of a million miles away. In about 1980 the first lunar excursion rocket will have set out with a hundred brave souls, some of them courageously sure they won't return to earth alive and indeed may not even be set down safely on the moon. But they will, and they will become the best salesmen possible for more visitors to the moon. Result: tourism will be second only to science as the principle activity on the moon in 2001. Actually the two pursuits will go hand in hand in this case, for when visitors see the advantages in the unique environment of the moon, they will be more convinced of the rightness of going there in the first place and spending the huge sums necessary to set up shop—including Lunar City with its Lunar Hilton dominating the moonscape, and the acres of clear plastic bubbles that make breathing possible for humans.

Getting to the moon is half the fun—and going home is the other half, jokesters add. So whatever happens *on* the moon will surely be the biggest bonus yet offered in travel and entertainment. Just walking on the moon will be worth the price of a ticket. Taking thirty-foot leaps across the sandy soil will be a dreamlike thrill, as will performing under low gravity on a trampoline or soaring about on tiny stubs of wings under a fifty-foot-high plastic bubble of air. Looking up at earth and the rest of the celestial bodies, including a peek through a large telescope unhampered by any atmospheric twinkling, will give viewers an idea of what this can mean to the scientists. Watching a mine being worked on the moon, and seeing the ore being fired to earth from a long launching rail, will be more thrilling when seen from a mile away than on television 240,000 miles from the scene.

Industrial operations that will be entertaining to watch will be cold welding and vapor deposition of integrated circuits in the moon's vacuum—especially for the industrialist who dreams of moving to the moon with his own work. For mountain climbers it will be the thrill of a lifetime to climb one of the mountains of the moon—some of which vault thirty thousand feet into the black sky and can be scaled by weird, unbelievable techniques because of low gravity and vacuum.

Participation sports are not what some people want; They get their thrills by gambling, which will be even bigger business in 2001. Las Vegas will be the model for a number of "fun cities" that flourish throughout the country and the world. Various schemes of government-run gambling will have been tried and abandoned, as were pioneering attempts at state lotteries decades earlier. But government will continue to tax gambling heavily, evoking little complaint.

The young people will very likely celebrate 2001 with the New Age Rock, a dance that will shake their elders to their aging foundations, although probably no more than they in their time startled their own parents. Music will be primarily random, programed by real-time computers for the most part, and danced in just as random and unpatterned a fashion. Older folks won't bother to invade the dance floor any more because of the scoffing they encounter for their courageous efforts.

People will still indulge in smoking and drinking, but drug addiction will have been all but eliminated because of the dangers to the user, his offspring and society in general. New and wildly hallucinating drugs will be discovered and used illicitly, but users of them will be a small minority, eventually caught up by the law and in most cases rehabilitated.

We will find more people engaged in the arts, but fewer bonafide artists. Whether this is good or bad depends on one's viewpoint. With more time to do it, more people will dabble in painting, poetry and sculpture. There will be fewer novelists, and fewer still writers of nonfiction, since such material will be handled largely by television in 2001.

Reading will still be much enjoyed, however, particularly since one can request any book in the world and get it on the TV screen in an instant in English translation or have it read aloud by an optical scanner. One possible innovation is "agumented" classics with Shakespeare and other old favorites computer-programed so they seem to have the slant of another writer, or the vernacular of any period desired by the listener.

The suggestion has been made that a big change will come in our lives as a result of not having to work so hard or so long. Instead of being plasterers or lawyers, for example, we may refer to ourselves primarily as mountain climbers, or hunters, or skindivers. In other words, our avocations and hobbies will be the really important part of our lives. To be sure, there will be some for whom work remains the most important part of their lives, but these will be people like statesmen, artists and novelists. The workaday engineer, plumber or bus driver will have three days a week, a month or two a year, and perhaps all his life after age fifty to indulge in painting, writing, skiing, flying or some other leisure pursuit. Man's destiny cannot be slavery to a machine or to the wants of the public.

By 2001 there should be far fewer people sick and tired of their jobs and less boredom and tedium connected with work. Absenteeism should decline, since there will be more time for relaxation between work days and work weeks.

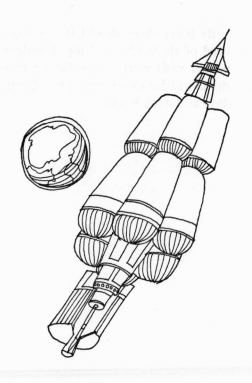

10 Space Travel

Let's look more closely at space travel from the serious scientific standpoint. The space age—inner and outer —began about the middle of the twentieth century. By the beginning of the twenty-first century both will be flourishing, to the good fortune of civilization as a whole and to the dismay and discomfort of those who felt that both ventures were wild-eyed science-fictioneering.

We've already visited the moon as tourists and seen something of what will be accomplished at that way station to true outer space. Predictably, in retrospect we will be able to say that the moon was first trod by man in 1970; by 1972 a permanent base was established and doing scientific research; commercial ventures began in 1975, closely monitored and controlled by their governments; the first moonchild was born in 1981 and is now just twenty years old; in 1972 spaceships landed astronauts on Mars and by 1973 orbited Venus.

In 2001 a colony on Mars will continue to be maintained, although the assignment is for only short periods of time. Although Venus is uninhabitable by man, robots continue to probe the planet.

Nuclear-heated chemical rockets will be used on space flights within the solar system. Nuclear energy will generate power for electrostatic drives probing into deep space. These drives, while providing very low thrust and acceleration, have tremendous duration, and thus can drive large craft far out into the galaxy at speeds that eventually reach millions of miles an hour.

Even at this speed, it takes years to get anywhere. The "deep freeze for deep space" will be standard procedure when human crewmen go along. Not surprisingly, there will be losses of life in such hazardous undertakings, just as the first airplane attempts to cross earth's seas resulted in tragedy. Some deep-space craft will vanish without a trace; some may be tugged into the sun and disappear in a flash of vapor; some will survive flights of many years and bring their crews back safe and sound, if somewhat older. By 2001 a huge unmanned space probe, built on the moon and fueled with lunar material, may be enroute to Alpha

Centauri in the hope of finding planets that are inhabited by intelligent life forms.

For a scientific technology that can mount such expeditions, flights to the moon, Mars and Venus will be simple in 2001. With nuclear power and sophisticated landing instruments, rocket ships will blast off from earth directly to the landing field at Lunar City. Most runs will be commercial and manned by airline pilots who have moved up to the coveted rank of Astro Commanders. Even scientific personnel and supplies for their laboratories on the moon will go commercial, although the Space Agency will still operate occasional flights to the moon and continue its research work with orbital and space flights from the moon.

Spaceports will be located on oceans some distance from shore to keep the mighty roar of their launching rockets from deafening the populace and to minimize the danger of explosion and nuclear radiation. These safeguards will justify the added expense and time involved in hauling passengers by boat from the mainland.

Space flight, like other forms of transportation, will be computerized, although on occasion well-trained crews will demonstrate that if necessary mere man can still make a manual landing on the moon or avoid a collision while en route. However, computer control is more precise and far less wearing on the space crew, and this is true also in the case of aircraft and high-speed surface transport. Flight personnel go along to monitor and to comply with regulations, as well as to qualify most passengers for the comforting and traditional image of the stagecoach driver, railroad engineer and pilot.

The population of the moon, while small compared with even the smallest of the American supercities, will nevertheless seem large when it is recalled that even scientists doubted that the cold, vacuum-packed ball in space could be colonized. Lunar City and its suburbs will house thousands of residents made up of a number of different categories of human beings. Pets are not included in the census, although there many will roam about happily on the moon.

Scientists will have been the first inhabitants, plus caretaking personnel for the various laboratories. Industry, not including the tourist trade, will account for most of the lunar population, with engineers, technicians, and their families in this bracket. Observers and researchers from various nations and from the United Nations add to the population. At any given time there are hundreds of visitors on the moon, straining the housing and eating facilities.

Some of the moon people will be those who simply prefer moon life to the earth and have retired on the moon. Some are here for medical reasons. Low gravity is easy on a tired heart, and some people have objections to replacing their original equipment with a stainless steel and plastic pump. A number of poets and novelists will settle on the moon, even at housing and food prices that would seem beyond the reach of those so traditionally underpaid. Painters and other practitioners of the arts will swell the total and do a thriving business in the souvenir trade.

Completing the total will be those who tend to the needs of others, including mechanics, shopkeepers, ministers, school teachers, communications people and salesmen. Lunar City will be the most cosmopolitan, most modern, of all cities in the solar system, even though it is one of the smallest.

Outside the city proper there will be few roads, since transportation in these areas is usually by rocket car instead of moonmobile. There will be outposts, scientific and industrial in nature, and in time there will be other cities like the pioneer Lunar City. Hotel chains will be building in such remote areas, counting on business trade and the desire of tourists for a longer look at local sights than the packaged tours give them.

Space Navigation

The mechanics of space travel will be well worked out by 2001. Navigation systems will rely on electronics and celestial sightings. Solar energy may provide electricity or heat for needed auxiliary equipment, and in some cases may even provide the prime motive power, as the solar wind pushes on huge solar sails of gossamer-thin material spun from lightweight masts in the zero gravity of space. Radiation hazards will be solved by careful monitoring of the sun and the use of shielding as necessary. When necessary, backup protection will be afforded by chemical injections to protect the cells of crew members from radiation.

Laser transmission may be used for powering spacecraft and orbiting stations, with a tight laser beam carrying energy to the receiver aboard such craft, eliminating the need for a weighty fuel tank and even for fuel itself! Consideration might be given to means of beaming solar energy in this way from the surface of the sun to the moon, or direct to earth or spacecraft as needed. Since a square yard of the sun's surface pours out something like 65,000 horsepower constantly, the advantages of this scheme become more obvious.

Space travel was at one time so minimal compared with air transportation and surface travel that pollution by spacecraft was no problem. However, with the tremendous increase in traffic in the last decades, space flights will have to be carefully policed and regulated. Spaceports will be relocated so that prevailing air currents in the atmosphere will quickly disperse pollutants. The earlier ferry flights to orbiting space stations may have to be resumed, with the main blastoff for the moon occurring there.

Inner Space

Man has been probing the depths beneath the sea for some time. In fact, the inventive Leonardo da Vinci dreamed up all sorts of equipment for primitive skin-divers, although he considered some of it so potentially useful for warmaking that he kept it secret with a code.

The invention of the aqualung made it possible for man to penetrate the depths untied to any umbilical cord of air connecting him with the world of air. Rubber fins transformed him into the fish with two tails, and special weapons made him a new predator of the deep. Mainly through the vision of Jacques-Yves Cousteau and his underwater colonies in the Mediterranean and elsewhere, it was proved that humans could survive and function hundreds of feet below the surface of the sea for weeks at a time. There remained only good reasons to accelerate the colonization of the sea and these reasons were found in the need for more food and other natural resources to care for an expanding, hungrier population.

As early as the 1950s scientists proved that animals from rats to dogs could learn to breathe water and extract the oxygen under certain conditions. In the 1960s a plastic film technology was developed for extracting oxygen from sea water, and by the late 1970s the "aquagill" was developed. By 2001 we will see that this simple breathing device has converted man into an underwater creature. Where scuba gear was limited in endurance and range by the size of its air tank, the gill now strains air from the surrounding sea, and a man-fish can remain below the surface as long as he cares to.

Anyone who starves in the ocean from now on will deserve it, and since the gill provides fresh water as well as air to its user, the problem of underwater survival by century XXI has been completely taken care of. Far more easily than man could survive on the moon, skindivers can go to the bottom of the continental shelf and remain there to play, to work, or to do scientific research. In our projection of the year 2001, thousands of men and women are doing all three. Let's take them in that order.

Adventure seekers dive merely for the pleasure of the experience, floating through a beautiful world beneath the surface, where strange and colorful things abound. Others, hunters at heart, enjoy the excitement of the chase, the kill and the repast. A requirement for membership in the Bottomscratchers, a pioneer California club of the 1930s was to capture a sandshark with the bare hands and bring it to the surface. Rugged as this feat was, it cannot match the sport of undersea hunting in 2001.

Motorized diving will be popular in hundreds of resorts around the world, from California to Florida and the Mediterranean; from Ceylon to South Africa and South America. With nuclear-heated wet suits the hardier adventurers will dive even in the waters of Antarctica, and whales and sharks will be ridden for hundreds of miles for sport and in the interest of science. For many, skindiving is a dream come true in living color. For others it provides a pleasant occupation—farming the sea, perhaps, or prospecting the ocean bottom for vital minerals.

In 2001 the fish farmer, who originally worked only at the very edges of the shore, lives hundreds of feet down and miles off shore. His herds are giant schools of fish, his tools electric prods and sonic signaling equipment. When his skilfully tended schools of fish are ready for market, he calls for a boat to pick them up for fileting on the spot.

Nature is prodigal with fish eggs, providing thousands and millions more than will live to maturity. The fish breeder of the twenty-first century protects the eggs he purchases and gets a yield far greater than nature ever expected. With the rich nutrients of the ocean depths, the fish crop multiplies faster than any dry-land animal herd possibly could. Farming the sea is exciting sport too, with a trained dolphin for a cowpony, and predator sharks to fight to make life interesting. Home is a plastic bubble anchored to the sandy bottom, fitted with as many comforts of home as the farmer wants—heat and light, a comfortable bed, reading material, and perhaps some music for the soul. It's a way of life once enjoyed by the kind of men who pioneered on dry land.

Another kind of man-fish will be a miner. He too will

live on the sea bottom for months at a time, but in larger quarters and with many more of his kind. Minerals abound all over the earth, but much of that earth is covered by water. Extending the diggings just to the continental shelves about the globe will consist simply in scraping the ocean bottom. There is oil and gas to be found too, and skindivers will guide the work of surface drilling ships as they probe for the rich pockets of these fuels.

Scientists will live beneath the waves too. Part of global weather prediction and control stems from knowledge of the temperature and movement of the seas; how better to get this information than to go to the source? Scientific groups will drill and study cores at the ocean bottom instead of hauling them laboriously to the surface. Marine biologists will study their flora and fauna on the spot, and archaeologists will probe the clefts and ridges of mountains invisible from above.

Many men will go down to the sea in 2001, not all of them in ships. Many will do it in swimfins and gills to open a vast new world for exploration—so vast that we will still know less about it than we know about the moon!

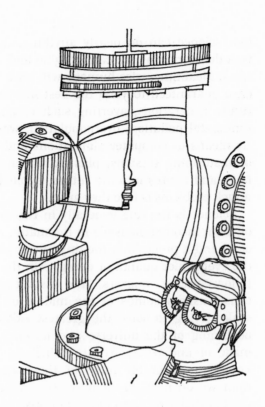

11 Science

In 2001, one of the U. S. cabinet posts will be that of Secretary of Science, and science will be a full-fledged member of the partnership of skills and abilities that run our country and plan its future. Although it is impossible to direct pure science, government will attempt to do those things we should do, and not merely what we *can* do—because by 2001 it will be evident that science can do nearly anything. In time it may well do everything we can imagine and a lot more besides. Meantime, wise humans will set a course for science guaranteed to yield the best life for present and future generations, averting such castrophes as environmental pollution, overpopulation, war and disease. By means of computer simulations and man-machine brainstorming sessions, plus extrapolations of known facts and figures into the future, applied research can attack problems before they arise.

Science is working generally in two directions, both of them incomprehensible in the matter of size. On the one hand it probes into the tiny nucleus of matter, and the even tinier quanta of energy. On the other hand it follows racing "quasars" into distant space. Human consciousness stands at the middle of this vast size scale, trying to solve the greatest riddles of all; the beginning of the universe and its end; what we are made of and where we are going. By 2001 we will know immeasurably more of these knotty problems than we do now, yet it may seem that we are even further than ever from final solutions.

The Unity of Science

Science will be more consciously directed and focused in 2001, and it will be also more unified than it is now. There was a time long ago when one scientist could know all the scientific lore gained up to his time. Then, of necessity at first, scientists began to divide science into tiny disciplines that for ages were maintained as separate entities, pure and untainted. Man succeeded in specializing science for his own convenience or aggrandizement into some 1,150 different disciplines, ranging in the English language from acarology to zymurgy. The reverse procedure, the integration of disciplines, began in earnest in the twentieth century. Then, as computers and electronics and human engineering flourished, it was found that disciplines overlapped and merged and became indistinguishable one from another. In electronics, for example, physicist, chemist and engineer have had to merge their knowledge. The "new" science of bionics is not new at all but rather a merger of biology and many branches of engineering, to the benefit of both the living and the nonliving systems of things.

Einstein sought until his death to unify the theories of gravity, electricity, and magnetism. In 2001 the search will go on. If the basis of the entire universe is nothing more nor less than a quantum of energy or a particle of matter the science governing its actions and interactions must be basically as simple. But it is terribly difficult to reach this plain of simplicity, and we seem able to do it only by climbing tortuous mountains and wandering into deep chasms far from our course.

Science and the Computer

The computer is a great unifying force. Industry, education, entertainment and transportation benefit from computers, and even more so does science. This is true for a number of reasons. Mathematics has been called the queen of sciences; surely it is its heart. And if there is a way to speed mathematics it speeds all science. Statistical results form the basis for many experiments. Statistics are handled rapidly and accurately by computers, and in quantities impossible by older hand calculation methods. Studies of genetics, nutrition and disease profit by computer analysis.

We have examined weather prediction and control in some detail. An Englishman named Richardson dreamed of such a system long ago but failed for one reason: lack of manpower. Using a battery of human assistants, he could put together a fairly accurate prophecy of the weather for the following day. But it took him several days to make the prediction! Weather computers now handle millions of bits of data in a given amount of time, but in 2001 they will be handling *billions* of bits in the same time—data assembled from all over the world and from every kind of weather monitor available, from surface craft, permanent stations and human readings to orbiting satellites, including the moon. All this information the computer can process and act on in the wink of a human eye. Then it draws a weather map, makes a spoken recording, and prints out a thick volume of data to supplement its work.

Computer "simulation" is also a powerful tool for everyone, including economists, meteorologists and space engineers. What effect will the opening of a new plastics factory in Europe have on the economy of Nigeria two and a half years from now? Would an additional sales tax of one-half per cent on Britons tend to disrupt the stability of trade in the West Indies? If so, what counteracting measures might be taken in the Indies or elsewhere so as not to reflect any feedback in the British economy?

There are two ways to find out these things. One is the way it was done before the computer: put the idea into practice and either help or hurt the economy. Then either pat yourself on the back or return to the drawing board for another idea in hope of saving the situation. Simulation allows the planner to try out his idea painlessly, and in a fraction of the time it would take in real life. At last politics can become the true science of government.

Another use for the scientific computer is information retrieval. It has been common industrial practice to "reinvent the wheel" or whatever else was necessary, provided the process did not cost more than $100,000 —a figure established by the cost of searching the literature to see if the work had already been done. There are classic examples in scientific history. Gregor Mendel worked out his genetics laws with plants, yet his paper gathered dust in the university library while two other men did the same work years later, only finding Mendel's after completing their own. Charles Darwin and Alfred Russel Wallace each formulated the same theory of evolution without knowing that another person was involved in the same project. There are times, of course, when independent effort is fine; but there are more times when knowing that a particular problem has been solved, and how, can save us precious time and effort better used to advance the project to the next step.

Science was drowning in a sea of published work when the computer appeared. The problem was not that there was no information but that there was too much. Every hour in the 1960s saw the publication of enough scientific literature to fill a ten-volume encyclopedia, but this material was scattered in dozens of lands, in dozens of languages, with no central clearing house. By 2001, compartmentalization of knowledge is a primary job of the computer and it has been done well.

Research results on any subject are available at the push of a button. A standard cataloging system with automatic translation into any of the several major scientific languages produces a wealth of information from the highspeed printer seconds after interrogation. The information is highly selected, too, and not just an outpouring of tons of data that will still be impossible to sift in time to be of use.

All the information that has been published on gravity waves, for example, would fill many volumes and be repetitious, so computer research will present information at a series of different levels: first, an abstract within one day of being up to date on the state of the art; second, a listing of key articles; third, a listing of secondary articles; fourth, a bibliography of all that has been published *and accepted* on the subject. Acceptability is of great importance.

In 2001 there is less such repetition of effort—less rehashing in different words. The old dictum of "publish or perish" no longer prevails. The computer sifts, selects and rejects. But there is still duplication of effort and much walking of the same mile, simply to be sure.

In 2001 a researcher interested in developing a new polymer for the chemical industry will begin with a search of patents and of literature on the subject. Research will yield a shelf of material many feet long but so well indexed and summarized as to make assimilation possible in a short time. If the problem is complicated enough the scientist may well assign to the computer the problem of seeking out the new molecular structure and methods of producing it.

Finally, when the project is complete, the computer will take on another onerous chore for its human partner—that of producing the technical paper for scientific journals. Sifting through all the data, the computer will compile the pertinent material, edit it, make an abstract and title it properly to fit the storage files on the subject. The scientist will merely look over "his" report, O.K. it, and move on to the next project.

Random Discoveries

A 2001 scientific research technique involving the computer will be "programed serendipity," with all computers at all times on the alert for useful chance discoveries. Many great inventions have come about by accident, but how many slip by? How many are not noticed until after several occurrences? We will program the computer to be on the lookout not just for what is sought, but for anything that might be useful. Often when the serendipity program turns up such a find, human brains won't grasp it at first. It may often be thought that the computer has goofed until a board of several people manages to grasp the discovery the electronic bloodhound is pointing out.

In 2001 science will be accepted for what it is: as natural as nature, as moral as mathematics, and as beneficial as raindrops and sunshine.

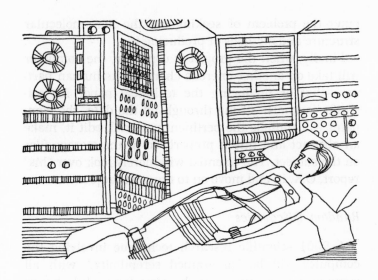

12 Health

By 2001 most diseases will be under control. Cancer, for example, will have been beaten. Influenza and malaria will be ancient history. Heart disease will be a minor problem, only partly because of the great and continuing success of transplants and artificial organs. One reason for this improvement in health will be the better environment we live in by then. Smog will be greatly curbed and much less a contributor to respiratory ills. Tobacco will still be smoked, but lung cancer will be all but wiped out. Tobacco itself will be treated to remove the carcinogenic, or cancer-producing, agents; but in addition, drugs and other therapy will be so effective that only periodic examinations will be necessary. Perhaps a vaccine will offer protection.

With methods like irradiation sterilization, harmful insects and organisms will be eliminated without the introduction of dangerous drugs into food, water and atmosphere. With the pollution of our air and water reduced by intelligent waste disposal processes, much of the danger to health will be removed. In fact, by 2001 medical science may have eliminated just about all diseases except for the common cold. And that will be so well-controlled that it will be only a nuisance and seldom progress to a more severe illness.

After many horrifying experiences with the effects of hallucinogenic drugs on the users and their offspring, a strong campaign of legislation, education and scientific treatment will all but eliminate such abuses.

Starting at the beginning—with the birth of a child —let's see how health will be safeguarded in 2001. Prenatal tests will seek out defects in the unborn child, and treatment will be given to rectify them. After birth, follow-up tests such as the PKU, or phenylke-tonuria, test are made. Birth defects, including mental retardation will be greatly reduced, and more of them will be corrected when they appear. Only a tiny pro-portion of the baby crop in 2001 will be seriously affected by any flaws. Periodic injections or oral doses of vaccines will prevent or mitigate the childhood dis-eases that once plagued us. Better nutrition will fur-ther strengthen the growing youngster.

Life expectancy in the developed countries will be

85 for girls and 78 for boys. Furthermore, the later years of life will be useful, happy ones and not a period of invalidism with the patient kept alive only by constant medical care. A simple approach to this problem is to identify the causes of death in the order of their lethal effects and then eliminate those causes.

One of the most diligently researched aspects of life will be that of aging. Why do we grow old, and is it inevitable? Men still die, even if they are not attacked by viruses. Hearts wear out, and so do the blood vessels that circulate the vital fluid. The brain deteriorates, as do the joints and bones themselves. By 2001, science may have found some of the reasons and learned to slow the process, if not arrest it entirely, by means of drugs or other therapy—including, perhaps, radiation.

Replacement Parts

Even in a completely sterile, disease-free world peopled by hardly individuals who are genetically sound and properly nourished, there will occasionally be accidents that damage their bodies. By 2001, someone who is accident prone or very unlucky just might arrive at old age completely rebuilt!

In 2001 the patient needing a new heart will have several choices. He may elect to take a donor heart from someone who has died, although such hearts will be scarce because fewer people will die of other causes. Or he may choose a culture-grown heart from the heart bank. They will be available in many sizes. The same will be true of kidneys, liver, spleen and stomach. In fact, just about anything but a brain will be available.

Alexis Carrel took a sliver of chicken heart and made it grow in the test tube. Scientists in 2001 will take a heart cell, grow it into the whole organ, and then put the spare part "on the shelf" until needed. Kept in cryogenic storage, it need not be kept alive in the normal sense of the word. In fact, it will be better that it not be functioning and thus wearing itself out.

The idea of test tube babies has raised ethical, moral and religious objections, but test tube spare parts will not be nearly so controversial. Substitute parts will be in stock in the hospital or in a nearby storage bank for quick delivery and implantation. Chemical treatment or radiation will guard against rejection of the new organ, which will be accepted by any person needing it, regardless of race, color, blood type, or any other qualification. In addition to vital organs, the spare-part bank will provide just about anything needed: hair, eyes, skin, bone, cartilage, blood, blood vessels, teeth, nerves, organs, joints, marrow.

As early as 1963 organs from chimpanzees were transplanted into men. In 1968 a pig's heart valve was used to save the life of a young woman. A pig's heart is about the right size for a person. In 2001 there may be animals specially bred to provide livesaving replacements.

A fourth replacement possibility will be the artificial organ or part. The artificial heart, once thought likely to succeed sooner than the living replacement, will have caught up to the transplant and probably be more popular with patients. There will be a good reason for this popularity: a heart of steel and plastic will never wear out. Neither will an artificial kidney. These later organs, once giant affairs to which the patient was "plugged in" for elimination of wastes in the blood, will be small enough for permanent implantation in the patient.

The artificial kidney can be considered a passive organ, since it simply filters poisons from the blood circulated through it. For the artificial heart, which requires power to operate its pumps, a number of sources are possible, including internal and external batteries that may be recharged as needed, a radio-active electrical generator that lasts for years, an air motor that uses the patient's breathing, and bioelectricity generated in the body tissues.

Entire limbs have been grafted onto injured patients, but because of the difficulties involved in matching the graft to the rest of the body for appearance, and the technical problem of hooking up all the vessels and nerves for proper operation, artificial limbs will be very much preferred in 2001. There will be a great difference in these, however. The great promise of Russian "myoelectric" hands and arms of the late 1950s will come true by 2001 and amputees will have artificial limbs that move in response to their own nervous systems. Even fingers will operate in this way, and "feedback" systems will make the prosthetic devices almost like real limbs. Arms and legs will be permanently attached by means of metal or plastic joints implanted in the body of the patient. It will be rare to see an amputee not fitted with a working and lifelike artificial limb.

Another possibility, which may make the electronic limb seem a last desperate resort, is the growing of a new arm or leg by the person who sustains the loss of a limb. Some lower animals, like the salamander, do this with no difficulty and it is conceivable that by 2001 science will have learned how to restart the planning and growing mechanism in the cells to replace the missing part.

The Deep Freeze

The use of hypothermia, or deep cooling of the body, for operations and also to put the patient into suspended animation for long periods, will be standard procedure in 2001. This will permit extensive surgery, rest and time for the strengthening of damaged or weak organs. The practice of deep-freezing incurables will continue, looking to the day when new techniques can bring them back to normal life. It is quite probable that a few adventurous souls will be using this method to give themselves a taste of immortality.

While science will not have learned the secret of eternal life by 2001, a deep-frozen body apparently will stay in suspended animation and be capable of being brought to life by warming, with no permanent damage even to the brain. The technique will be used in long space flights, as we have noted, and astronauts will safely "sleep" for periods of years with no apparent harm to any part of their bodies. One problem that may be raised by this procedure is whether or not they are entitled to pay and allowances. To all effects they will not be working (they won't even breathe!) and they will need no allowance for food and drink.

A Healthier World

With the lengthening of the natural life span and the saving of the lives of far more injured people, the population of the world was bound to increase greatly. Because it was inhuman to save lives only for slow starvation, birth control finally became a reality. In what will be considered drastic measures, entire populations in the future will be kept normally sterile by drugs. Children will be conceived only if antidotes are consciously taken to counteract the sterilizing drugs. The mortality rate of young children will drop rewardingly, particularly in underveloped lands, so that most of them will grow up to enjoy the good health science had succeeded in bringing to the world.

The elimination of disease will come through wiping out germ carriers, vaccinating everybody, and improving the environment through smog control and other pollution curbs. The danger from increasing radioactivity caused by weapons testing and industrial and other peaceful uses of nuclear blasts will be minimized in 2001 by making chemical protection against radiation available to everyone.

The scientific world has known for many decades that genetic mutations can be induced with chemicals and with radiation, but most of those that occur naturally are harmful—sometimes fatal, and sometimes render the mutant incapable of producing normal offspring. However, with greater knowledge of biochemistry, science will be on the verge of altering the genetic structure of the cell to remove inherent weaknesses in the human body—and, perhaps more importantly, the human mind.

Much progress will have been made in mental health. Continuing research will prove that mental disease is caused by organic flaws in body chemistry. Through proper diet and corrective drugs, and sometimes through surgery, ailing minds will be restored. Crime will be reduced by this approach, since criminal tendencies show up early in a person's chemistry.

With the great reduction in diseases, authorities will concentrate on accident prevention. The highway death and accident toll will be reduced by the development of better automobiles, highways, and regulations, plus curbs on drunk and reckless driving. For better care of those who still are injured in accidents, medical authorities will adopt techniques proved valuable in wartime medical evacuation, using helicopters or VTOL aircraft to rush victims to hospitals.

As we have seen in an earlier chapter, the computer will prove to be an accurate medical examiner and diagnostician and in routine cases will deal directly with the patient at the clinic. Sample analyses and writing of prescriptions will be natural tasks for the medical computer, while the human practitioner devotes more of his time to surgery and to biological research. However, although much success will have been attained with test tube experimentation, living human beings will still not be artificially created from the raw elements of nature, despite the optimism of some scientists and the obvious logic of their claim that the principle of creating life from nonlife has already been proved.

13 Food

As visitors from an earlier day to 2001, we will notice first that the main difference in food will be in the packaging. Little food will be bought in bulk in the United States; nearly everything will come in meal-sized boxes, cans, jars, or just plain plastic sacks. Most dinners will be TV dinners, except that few will be frozen and most will be excellent. Foods sterilized and preserved by irradiation can be kept at room temperature and prepared more quickly for the table. For weight-watchers there will be special packaged meals treated with appetite-curbing drugs to insure that no more is eaten than is required.

Although the mythical food pills of science-fiction stories will not replace natural foods by 2001—no complete steak-and-potatoes meal with dessert will be compressed into a capsule the size of a cold tablet—there will be many concentrated foods and liquid diets for those on the run or toothless. It is possible to put the proper nourishment into such a diet, but the human gastrointestinal tract remains much as it was when we subsisted on wild grasses, nuts and berries. A certain amount of roughage will be necessary if we are to function properly with the equipment we have.

In 2001 there will be six billion mouths to feed, an increase of a hundred percent over those eating today. Achievement of the goal of a nourishing diet for all the world will mean the tripling of the food supply by 2001. The food-shortage problem is tied inseparably to industrial development in the undeveloped lands. Until some of the eighty percent of the population now needed to provide food for such nations can be shifted to industry, no progress can be made.

Each farmer in the United States can produce enough food for thirty people. Mechanization, chemicals, breeding and feeding have been responsible for doubling the output from an acre of land and cutting the need for farm workers sevenfold in this country. Since most arable land is now being used throughout the world, further increases in production must be made as it has been made in the civilized countries—

by more efficient methods of conventional farming and stock raising.

Dirt Farming

In 2001 there will be more mechanization of farm land in the less developed countries, and more chemicals will be used for enriching the soil and for killing pests that previously wrecked crops. A mere dozen varieties of the 12,000 known species of plants are used for most of the food today; by 2001 there will be others to make better use of certain soils, climates and food needs. Such techniques as "chemical tillage," in which chemicals are added to the soil instead of ploughing, may be adopted.

Because of water shortages, there will be more use made of salt-tolerant crops. This will permit the irrigation of farms near the shore with sea water and open up acreage previously unavailable for crop production.

The mechanical picking of crops, which has proved to be better, faster, and cheaper than "stoop labor," will free workers from the farm and make them available for other endeavors, including manufacturing, which can increase the economy of a country.

Seen from the air, the most modern dirt farms of 2001 will look like huge squares and rectangles of plastic—and that is what they will be. Acreage will be enclosed in a canopy of clear plastic, most of it supported by air pressure. Inside we will find the atmosphere steamy, and in some cases we will have to don oxygen masks to breathe, because additional carbon dioxide has been pumped into the farm's atmosphere.

Why grow everything in such a hothouse, and how can a farmer afford the added expense? The main reason is water.

Water crisis or not, man will see to it that he has plenty in 2001. But it costs money. To desalinate takes energy, and energy costs dollars. In areas where free fresh water is not available for agriculture, or where it is not available very cheaply, the farmer must conserve the expensive liquid. On farms of yesterday, ninety-eight percent or more of the water used in irrigation was wasted, either as runoff or in evaporation. Now the atmosphere extends only a few feet above the crops, and water that evaporates is trapped in the system. It condenses on the plastic covers and runs back down, to be used again and again.

Plastic keeps in water vapor and it also keeps in heat. That is why we find the humidity uncomfortably warm. Added carbon dioxide stimulates plant growth, too, and we'll find crops on an average farm that we would normally look for only in a lush humid jungle. There are additional benefits under the plastic sky. Birds and insects can't get at the harvest, and weeds are kept out, too. Of course it costs money to buy and maintain the plastic, to pump air and CO_2 into it. But with greatly increased yields and less water consumption, the result is more products and profit.

Water Farming

Food can be produced by other methods than dry farming, and space travel will accelerate such research. One of these is "hydroponics," the growing of crops in tanks of chemicals or in gravel beds saturated with nutrients. While there may be limited use of this method it will not account for an appreciable part of the world's output. The moon will be a better prospect for hydroponics. Algae culture will fare better.

Pioneered in the mid-twentieth century, the culture of algae offered a great potential in high yield per acre. Algae don't need good soil; in fact, they need no soil at all. The organisms are grown in a circulating medium of water and nutrients. In the 1960s a plant in Osaka, Japan was producing more than fifty pounds of algae a day. However, the process was expensive and the product did not meet with wide acceptance in vital matters of aroma and taste.

After years of indecisive results, by 2001 the proponents of algae culture will have hit on the right strains of palatable organisms and be able to harvest them economically from huge tanks of water. Operating on a continuous basis, with no weeds, leaves or other waste, the greenish growth that is a nuisance to lakes and swimming pools will be a profitable and nutritious food, sold as an additive for flour, soup, and other foods. It will also be made into puddings and meat substitutes.

But—to risk a pun—algae culture is merely skimming the surface of the water. The real revolution must take place in the ocean; the old dream of harvesting or farming the sea must come true. Historically, fishermen have been only hunters, and until science learns how to manipulate the "food chain" between plankton and large fish to best yield calories for human consumption he will not truly be farming the sea. Used as meat, vitamins, and a powdered additive to other foods, this protein from the ocean is a valuable supplement to meat from land animals. Seaweed will be harvested for food, along with other marine life down to and including plankton, the almost microscopic organisms that are the basis of food in the sea. It is estimated that by putting out more fishing fleets we could increase our fish catch as much as four times without going to fish farming operations.

Most fish farming is now limited to rice paddies and shallow waters, where it is easy to tend the schools of new fish. Yields of three hundred pounds of fish an acre are achieved in this way, even without feeding the fish. By adding feed this can be upped to two thousand pounds per acre. By 2001 the techniques of fish farming will have improved and been extended to more "acreage." With scientific help for nature in producing more from its prodigal output of eggs, the food supply from the sea will be greatly augmented.

Cheap, available calories and proteins will be included in diets as additives and enricheners. Soy beans, corn, green leafy vegetable derivatives, algae and fish will provide much of the necessary food additives, and grain and flour will be enriched with synthetic amino acids. Alfalfa is also being considered as a source of amino acids, since its yield is up to three hundred pounds per acre, in comparison with only ninety pounds of rice. Fish meal, finally given a clean bill of health by the U. S. Food and Drug Administration, will contribute to the world's food supply as an additive. Entire fish are ground up to make the meal at a price low enough to be available to poor nations.

Supplements and Substitutes

Food production throughout the world will have to be improved with technical know-how from developed countries, but also with new ideas. Even among the undeveloped countries with problems of malnutrition people are choosy about what they eat and sometimes go hungry when there is a good supply of nourishing—but not very palatable—food at hand. The problem is to shift eating habits to take best advantage of the supply at hand.

Most people would prefer a high-protein diet, largely from meat, which is standard fare in the United States and other developed countries. This is also the most expensive kind of diet, with regard to the drain on available food. Producing the meat for our tables costs several times the nutrition directly available in grain and other foods. As a general rule, only ten percent of the food consumed by meat animals becomes useful meat. Milk cows do somewhat better, turning almost twenty-five percent of their food into milk, rich in protein. And chickens yield as much as fifty percent in meat from the feed they eat.

A more efficient diet for people would be, of course, vegetables and grain instead of meat. The problem is to make these more readily available foods appealing to sophisticated taste buds. Progress is being made in this direction. In 1967, for example, General Mills, Inc. announced synthetic meats produced from vegetable matter. To make the new product, protein is first extracted from soy beans, using a mild alkali. The concentrated protein is next mixed with a solvent and forced through dies to make fine fibres, much as synthetic cloth is made. These protein fibres are then coagulated, or hardened, and blended with fat—either animal or vegetable. Flavor and color are added, and then the protein is mixed with egg albumen. The synthetic meat produced is similar to beef, poultry or sea food. It can be frozen, canned, or dehydrated for packaging. Since it is cooked during the processing, it can be eaten cold if desired.

Present meat substitutes are expensive to produce, but by 2001 they will be available at a fraction of the cost of real meat and perhaps will compete even in the developed countries with the real thing. At the very least they will make tastier meals within the reach of those with less money to spend.

There is a sad story about the farmer who taught his horses to eat sawdust by fitting them with green glasses. Unfortunately, just about the time they got used to the diet, they died. Nutritionists in 2001 will have better success in breaking down cellulose.

Experiments show that molasses can provide about three fourths of the dry food of cattle, thus making it possible to turn sweets into meat. Later, experiments were conducted in feeding waste newsprint, mixed with molasses, to cows. The bovines seemed to be able to digest the news satisfactorily; they thrived on their diet. Even stranger than the feeding of old newspapers was the use of termites as food. Termites eat wood, of course, and the theory was to let them digest the cellulose and convert it to protein, whereupon people could eat the termites. In 2001 a more direct approach will be taken, with paper-eating cows and wood-consuming termites bypassed completely.

In 1967 the industrial firm of British Petroleum announced that it had successfully raised pigs and chickens on protein in the form of yeasts. Yeast as a food is no novelty, but what was remarkable about the British announcement was that the yeast itself was grown on petroleum! Since man can eat pigs and chickens, the experiments demonstrated that indirectly man could live on petroleum. The same thing is true of paraffin and methane gas. And scientists in the United States at the Pittsburg Coal Research Center reported in 1966 that yeast could be grown on coal.

While there seems a problem in using fossil fuels for food if they are already dwindling, man will surely eat before he operates his machines. And it is comforting to know that even if all the food runs out we can still mine coal and live on it. Incidentally, if it is necessary to feed the world this way, it could be done with just three percent of the total that is consumed for fuel. And our diets would certainly contain plenty of minerals!

In addition to using new substances as animal fodder and as food additives, the world in 2001 may have to turn to using them as primary foods. Germany created new food products and a new word—*ersatz*—during wartime when conventional foods ran short. Sawdust and other waste products may be made to yield palatable foods by breaking them down chemically and converting them into nutritious foods people can eat.

Culture Farming

In 2001 industrial labs will grow meats and vegetables in huge vats. Tissue culture will include any cellular tissue man desires, from ham to tomatoes to lima beans. Growing around the clock all year long in a sterile environment, with nutritives added automatically in the process, meats and vegetables will be "harvested" and packaged for market on an assembly-line basis. Carefully monitored for flavor, tenderness, color and a host of other important characteristics, the cultured foods will match natural products in everything but shape. In some cases even that will be taken care of, and tissue will be cut or molded into familiar shapes for more customer appeal. However, many will enjoy meat served in standard rectangular slabs, much as an earlier generation enjoyed something called Spam in the shape of the can it came in.

Consider the advantages of cultured steak. In the tissue culture lab, all the product will be top-grade sirloin, T-bone, or pork chop—boneless, of course, and with no hooves, horns or hide to dispose of. Vegetables will offer the same advantages, with no leaves, seeds, stems or pulp.

In the laboratory, efficiency will be boosted many times and all the nutritives fed to the culture will end up as useful food product—a product not contaminated by germs that plague the real thing. Cultured ham will never give anyone trichinosis, for example.

Besides duplicating the texture and flavor of familiar foods, the tissue lab will create new taste thrills. Most of the big producers will have researchers constantly seeking for new discoveries to tickle the taste buds of customers. How about combining ham and eggs, for example, in one product? Or Cornish hen and wild rice? Blending the garlic right into the veal during production? And completely artificial food products can be created by combining a computer and biochemistry.

Much of the improvement in the food situation in

2001 will be simply through the preservation of food already on hand. Elimination of rats and other pests in Asia, for example, will add greatly to the supply of usable wheat and other grains. Extinction of screw-worm flies and other pests by irradiation to make them sterile will yield more cattle for food. And the irradiation of stored grains and other foods will cut down losses as well. To keep food long periods of time without freezing, widespread use will be made of techniques like freeze drying, vacuum drying, and "foam-mat" drying, the last particularly effective for fruit juices. Another method of food storage will be to exclude oxygen to prevent rotting. The addition of CO^2 has the effect of keeping oxygen out of stored food.

Despite the fears and warnings of many that the world will face starvation before the year 2001, its billions will be fed, and in better fashion than now. Malthus continues to be wrong. While there is, of course, a limit to how many humans can subsist on the food produced by our planet, we will not be near that limit at the turn of the century.

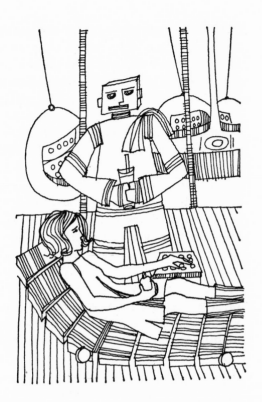

14 Fuel and Power

Primitive man managed to live on the energy in about three thousand calories of food. This is equivalent to several kilowatt-hours. Modern man has geared his life to many more kilowatt-hours than this, and during the time from now until 2001 he will use up three times as much energy as has been used in *all previous history*. This is significant because of a vital problem: There is a fixed amount of fuel of various kinds in the earth, and after that is used man will go power-hungry. This will not happen by 2001, however, although power consumption by then will make the present generation seem a nation of conservationists!

Man's first means of land transportation, aside from his own legs, was probably the horse, and his first extension of his physical power for industrial purposes may also have been the horse.

If we should use only a straight-line projection to 2001, total horsepower of machines then will be near 100 billion horsepower, and this figure is most likely low. Man will burn up a fantastic amount of fuel.

Presently, the greatest single use of energy is for heating, and this will probably still be the case in 2001. We use one-fourth or more of our fuel in the United States to keep warm. Year-round air-conditioning adds to the demand on fuel, and in hot countries it costs much more to cool in summer than to heat in winter. The author's utility bill more than doubles in summer, for example.

The odds are good that houses of 2001 will be even more electrified than those of today. Air-conditioning inside and out will be a factor, with perhaps even our clothes cooled and heated. There will be "robot" servants to clean house, make beds, and wash the car. Swimming pools will be more numerous, necessitating power systems for pumping, filtering, lighting, heating and cooling. Lighting, both in the home and on the grounds, will be an added factor. Computer service and more communication systems will also require more power.

Electric cars may be re-charged by home power

plants or public utilities. Transportation will eat up more fuel. Since it is not likely that we will live any closer to work or recreation areas in 2001 than we now do, more traveling will be done. Space travel, although still representing a small part of total fuel consumption, will require appreciably more power as more and longer flights are made.

While there will still be "haves" and "have nots" in 2001, the presently underdeveloped parts of our world will have proportionately more and thus create an added drain on waning stockpiles of fuels.

Before investigating how all this new power is going to be produced, let's take a quick look at power use in a typical city in the year 2001. We have mentioned the emergence of the individual power plant in homes some distance away from a central plant. A major reason for this, besides convenience and the safeguard against power failure during storm or other emergency, is that even a small fuel cell power plant can have a very high efficiency compared with conventional power supplies like gasoline or diesel engines. A large, fairly efficient steam power plant fueled either by fossil fuels or nuclear energy is too large and costly for a small area. Transmission charges add to the cost of power, too. Thus it is economically sound to install a self-sufficient power plant in many homes.

On a smaller scale, the same principle is bound to invade the power tool field. Batteries or other such sources will power tools like lawn mowers, eliminating unwieldy cords. The batteries will be recharged occasionally from a handy electric outlet, of course. Hair dryers, children's toys, record players and TV sets will be cord-free, as some few are already.

The Fuel Supply

Now let's see about power sources. Fossil fuels like coal, gas and oil make up the bulk of our energy supply, and worldwide they will still be doing it in 2001. But nuclear energy will then account for perhaps half the electric power in the United States and an appreciable share in other developed nations. In all probability there will be many nuclear-powered ships. There may be nuclear trains and airplanes as well, and nuclear-powered spacecraft for long missions. The nuclear automobile will not be a reality unless there is some unforeseen breakthrough. Considerations of safety and economy both work against using a small nuclear reactor in the midst of a large number of people. Most nuclear power plants will be suppliers of huge amounts of electric power for metropolitan areas or large industry.

Like fossil fuels, nuclear fuels are limited. However, they will still be available in 2001. While nuclear energy won't oust coal, oil and gas in all applications, it will help produce those fuels. Released as heat or pure energy, nuclear fuel has proved its ability to blast huge craters and caves. The pioneering "Project Gasbuggy" in the American Southwest recently prospected for gas, taking the place of conventional explosives and well-drilling equipment. This is a potentially safe and effective mining method. Nuclear blasts may not only dig down to mineral deposits but also break them up for easy handling at the same time.

Understandably, miners have sought the highest-quality coal deposits and the richest gas and oil finds. As these dwindle it will be necessary to exploit poorer deposits, and nuclear blast techniques may make such handling feasible. There are other schemes too, such as burning coal where it is found and tapping the heat produced, perhaps as steam—piped direct to a power plant.

Geothermal wells, like those that heat much of Iceland and provide electric power in Italy and California, will continue to be developed. While these will not serve many of the power needs of 2001, they will be exploited when found close enough to an area needing power. Water power and wind power also will be harnessed to a greater extent than now. Their "fuel" is free, although it may cost a bit to convert it into power. Such power plants are clean too, and will produce no smoke, ash, harmful effluent or radiation.

Tidal power today is in the "exotic" category, but in 2001 we will see more schemes in operation than the very few now producing power or planned, such as those at the Severn River Estuary in England, and at the River Rance and Mont St. Michel in France.

Power From the Sun

As the handful of solar energy enthusiasts know, a square yard of sunshine contains about one horsepower. It is quite easy to cook a meal, distill water or heat a house with sunshine. We don't do it because it is even easier to burn coal, oil or gas, or to turn on the electric switch. But in 2001 we will see more use of this power source that is clean, safe, simple and free. A government study made during World War II suggested that by 1985 there would be millions of homes heated by solar energy in the United States. In 1968 we are far behind schedule, with perhaps only a dozen such dwellings. But in 2001 we shall see many.

With much of our fuel going to heat our homes, the use of sunshine for this purpose makes good sense. Solar energy is largely heat, and this heat is easy to take advantage of. Low-cost solar heaters will consist simply of well-insulated walls, reflective panels, and a storage tank of water, as we saw in Chapter 2. During the day the reflective panels are rolled back, permitting sunshine to enter the attic and warm a tank of water. At night the panels slide shut and retain the warmth. In summer a similar sliding panel arrangement keeps out sunshine during the day and radiates away unwanted heat during the cool nights. In many areas such systems will take care of heating and cooling needs the year round with savings of much fuel. Of course, the ultimate source of the energy is the same whether we burn fossil fuel or tap the sun directly, because the sun created the vegetation that slowly turned to coal or oil during the long ages past.

Anchored offshore in southern waters will be a new kind of power plant. Called STE, for Sea Thermal Energy, this installation taps solar heat in another way to generate electricity for utilities. A conventional steam engine works on heat from a fuel. The STE engine uses a gas such as butane to convert the low heat from surface water to power. Warm water from the ocean surface is piped into the STE engine and heats the gas. This expands and drives a turbine, then is cooled by water taken from the depths of the sea. The cooled gas returns once more to be expanded by heat, and the cycle continues. A temperature difference of about forty degrees is used in the STE, compared with the several-hundred-degree difference in conventional power plants. This makes for a very inefficient plant, but since the "fuel" is free, the STE can operate economically. Best of all, it uses none of our limited fossil or nuclear fuels.

In the last chapter we suggested an aircraft powered by solar energy. There may also be small surface vehicles driven in the same way, using electricity from a rooftop solar panel. In 1968 solar cells cost several dollars a square inch, making them feasible only for space applications and solar-powered radios for hobbyists. With cheap, large-area panels producing electricity at an efficiency of ten per cent, it will be possible to generate power for many applications. We may find some homes entirely solar-powered, using solar heat for comfort and solar-produced electricity for other needs.

Solar energy may also be used in desalinating water. As early as 1891 a huge solar still in the Andes mountains produced thousands of gallons of fresh water a day in a remote area. Recently a number of more modern installations were made in the United States, Mexico, Australia and Greece. Although a solar still requires a vast area of land to produce any sizable amount of fresh water, it is fine for a remote area or an area of land not good for any other purpose. The still itself is simple to construct and maintain, uses no-cost fuel, and produces nothing but fresh water and salt, without the smoke and ash of conventional desalinating units.

There will be more unusual uses of solar energy to produce power in 2001. One example is a hydroelectric plant not far from the ocean, driven by water diverted into a canal that empties into a low-lying basin. There are a number of suitable sites. Here is how such a model plant, dug with nuclear energy charges, would work. As soon as the channel is opened, sea water rushes in to fill up the depression. The turbine turns merrily, producing electricity for the area. But what happens when the basin is filled to sea level? At first glance the project seems like some greedy politician's pork barrel, but let's look further. There are strong winds in this area, and as they blow over the new lake, water evaporates. To replace this, more must come in from the sea, of course, and this continues to drive the power plant!

Electricity—Universal Power Supply

Electricity is the most desirable form of power man knows of. It is easily shut off at the turn of a switch, stores readily in batteries, and can be transported through small-diameter wires. It is silent and odorless, with no smoke, ash or harmful residue. True, touching a "hot" wire can be a shocking experience, but so can touching a red-hot exhaust pipe or steam boiler.

Man's first electric generators were direct in nature. In the simple voltaic cell of Alessandro Volta, chemicals were changed directly into electricity. The output of power was low, however, and scientists learned how to produce more electricity by attaching steam or gasoline engines to electromagnetic generators. This approach prevailed, even though a primitive fuel cell was demonstrated more than a hundred years ago.

The internal combustion engine, or the steam engine —any heat engine, as a matter of fact—is doomed to a fairly low efficiency. In the case of a steam electric plant, the efficiency is less than forty per cent, and this is much better than that of an automobile engine. For higher efficiency, then, and also for simplicity, engineers belatedly went back to the direct conversion approach.

We have seen the solar battery in operation. It is an elegant example of the direct conversion of light into electricity. Heat can be converted too, as Thomas Seebeck demonstrated a century ago by heating a wire and producing current. Later it was learned that the same thermoelectric "junction" could be made to produce heat or cold, depending on which direction the current was sent through it. In the year 2001 we find not only thermoelectric generators but also devices using the thermoelectric effect in reverse, including refrigerators and heaters. One unit either heats or cools a home at the flip of a reversing switch.

"Thermionic" conversion is another approach to producing electricity. Heating one element of the "pile" creates a flow of electrons somewhat like that in the thermoelectric generator. Fueled with radioactive isotopes, such a direct converter finds many uses.

There is another converter called the magnetohydrodynamic generator, or MHD for shortness and ease. This is in effect an electronic steam engine, for it converts the energy of a plasma, or hot, charged gas, into a flow of current by moving it through the field of a magnet. Such generators have a higher efficiency and by 2001 will have all but superseded the old-fashioned steam electric plant. Heat for the plasma comes from either fossil fuels or nuclear fuel.

"Biopower"

For a long time engineers have exploited the efforts of tiny organisms of bacteria by burning the methane gas they produce to produce heat and power. A more sophisticated approach is to generate electricity in this manner, and 2001 may show us some applications of this "biopower,"—for example, a sewage-disposal plant powered by the electricity the bacteria themselves generate. The effluent from a sawmill generates useful amounts of biopower, and for maritime use there are similar generators that operate on sea water and a marine organism. In this way material useful as fuel in no other way is exploited.

Power Unlimited

The most recent survey, made in 2000, shows fossil fuels down to the point where they will last only a few more decades if used at the present accelerated pace. Even radioactive materials are beginning to become scarce, and there are searches being conducted all the time for new finds of uranium and other nuclear elements. Long ago a man named Malthus predicted that we would hit a "population barrier" shortly, because while man was increasing at a great rate his supply of food was limited rigidly. Malthus was wrong only because man found better ways to produce food. For the same reason the criers of doom with regard to fuel supplies were wrong. Let's take a trip now to the first commercial fusion powerplant in the world, one recently completed in the heart of SanSan, where its electricity is carried up and down the coast to millions of users.

Nuclear fission became a reality in 1938, and the first reactor was built in 1942. The first artificial fusion reaction was effected in 1952, although the sun has been doing it for billions of years. In fission, the nucleus is split apart and produces energy from matter; in fusion, the reverse process takes place. Two nuclei of deuterium, or "heavy water," fuse into one nucleus of hydrogen, with a tremendous amount of energy left over. Almost as soon as the first fusion bomb was fired, scientists began trying to build a device to harness the power of fusion. Unlike fission, fusion took a very long period of trial between destructive use and constructive application. Dozens of promising methods for generating plasma had been followed in programs like "pinch" the Stellarator, "magnetic mirror," Astron and Perhapsatron. Fusion requires fantastic temperatures. As one writer put it, the process is like trying to contain the flame from a welding torch in a balloon. But in 2001 the job was finally done.

Heavy water is an "isotope," a special atomic arrangement of water. Instead of normal hydrogen, this isotope has hydrogen with a nucleus containing a neutron in addition to a proton. Because of this, two deuterium atoms fuse to make a helium atom plus extra energy. If it were possible to accelerate deuterium to about the speed of light, and heat it to, say, $100,000,000°$ Centigrade, matter would be converted directly into electricity and man's power problems would be solved for the foreseeable future.

Let's fictionize such a discovery: After scientists have spent some sixty years in a fruitless search for a way to harness fusion, a young psysicist working on a completely different project stumbles onto the secret. His experiment is with gravity "waves" and involves a high-energy accelerator producing billions of electron-volts of energy. One evening he accidentally leaves the accelerator running. At midnight a time switch shuts it off for a split second and then fires it again. The resulting avalanche of electrons creates the hot plasma physicists had sought in vain, as the young scientist realizes in the morning, when he looks at his instrument recordings and the melted accelerator. Convincing his bosses not to fire him, the scientist contacts an expert in fusion research and within a week "Serendipity I" is producing more than a hundred gigawatts of power from refined sea water!

Since a gallon of water from the ocean produces the power yielded by 350 gallons of high-test gas, and there are quite a few gallons of ocean water available, it is calculated that at 2001 rates of consumption it will take several billion years to exhaust the fusion power supply. All of which makes the interesting other approaches to power of academic interest only.

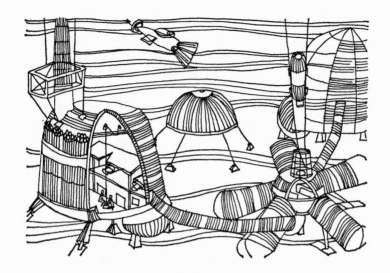

15 Natural Resources

Predictions have been made that the world faces early starvation; that there will be no water to raise crops; and that coal, oil and gas will be used up. In earlier chapters we saw that people will still be eating in 2001, and that engines will still run, too. In this chapter we shall look more closely into how man will hoard his natural reserves and guard against the pollution of air and water that threaten in the future. It is a never-ending fight to guard this treasure nature bequeathed us, but the fight must be waged and won if mankind is to prosper, or even to survive.

First and foremost we need clean air to breathe, or everything else is an exercise in wasted time. Next, man needs water to drink and food to eat. Finally, he requires fuels, minerals and a number of other substances. Let us hold to this order as we check the status of the stockpile of natural resources in 2001. Air is first on our agenda.

Clean Air

By 2001 the air pollution problem of today will be a dim and almost faded memory. There were tragedies caused by poisoned air long ago, notably in London, England, and in our own industrial areas. There will be others, but at some point ahead, smog will begin fading away.

Citizens will be so charmed by blue skies and beautiful mountain and seascapes they had almost forgotten that the process of cleaning the air will speed with the first evidences of success. Without question, the electric car will be the largest single contributor to the cleanup. Despite gloomy predictions of widespread unemployment and economic chaos with the wiping out of filling stations, gasoline and diesel-powered cars and trucks will be outlawed. After a period of near-revolt, the "smoggers" will be driven from streets and highways and locked up in impoundment centers. Those aged past a certain year will be scrapped for the metal in them. Some will be sold on the foreign market where smog is no problem, and some will be converted to electric power. Mostly, people will forget them and make do with the new "kilowatt karts." Surprisingly, these will be adopted almost immediately, and it will be hard to find a driver in 2001 who would go back to a gasoline buggy, although some sentimentalists will restore old cars by replacing the engines with electric motors. These whims will be tolerantly accepted by the rest of the driving public.

What happens to filling stations? There will still be a need for service; some cars will use quick-charge batteries, and stations provide this service. They will also sell replacement parts, tires, and of course fuel for fuel cell cars, of which there will be many. There may be as many stations as ever, as a matter of fact.

With perhaps half the power coming from the rails in the freeways, however, there will be less fuel sold in filling stations (particularly since fuel cells are more than fifty per cent efficient in converting liquid fuel to power). The oil companies, which used to make huge quantities of gasoline for the automobile trade, will now sell it to the power plants that provide electricity for the freeways. And since the mileage per vehicle will increase, they will sell more fuel than before.

Learning that life can be beautiful, and that it isn't necessary to weep and be plagued with bronchitis all the time, citizens will demand curbs on other foulers of the air. Pollutant rates will begin to drop all over the country as various cities compete with each other for blue sky.

Industry will learn that it can trap or precipitate most smoke and other pollutants. Often it will be found that burning is not necessary and that other chemical processes will do the job. The fuel cell, for example, has other uses than providing electric power and may become the backbone of many electrochemical industries. It emits no smoke, no ash—nothing but useful product and clean air all around the facility!

As in the case of the water problem, part of the solution will be to charge realistically for air pollution. When business—mining, for example—learns that it can't greedily exploit the atmosphere, it will find better and cleaner ways to get the job done. Many mines will produce no smoke at all, the ore-refining process being an entirely new one called "electrowinning."

About the only fire and smoke we will see in 2001 will come from campfires and backyard barbecues. These will be no problem after the tons of pollutants that once dirtied up our air have been removed. Smog control will be a large factor in the continuing growth of BosWash, ChiPitts, and SanSan. If residents can have the advantages of jobs, low cost housing, and beautiful skies besides, few will flee from the megalopolis.

Water

In 1965, two hundred million Americans used 350 billion gallons of water a day. In 2001 three hundred million Americans will use 1,400 billion gallons a day! If a crisis was impending earlier, what of the situation in 2001? Weathermakers will provide some additional water in the form of rain and snow, but this is not the entire answer. Desalination by a number of means will be part of the solution but a major step toward sufficient water for all, with an ample reserve for growth and emergencies, is the conservation of what water we have to begin with.

Far less water will be wasted in 2001. People will have learned its value, primarily because they will pay for it realistically and the cost will not be hidden in fixed rates or subsidies through taxation. A homeowner will see to it that he does not pay for a commodity that runs down the drain through leaky faucets or through sprinklers carelessly flooding the lawn. In fact, if water consumption jumps appreciably over his average for the last few months he will have a quick inspection visit from an official of the waterworks!

Artificial landscaping will permit attractive grounds with less work and less water consumption. Underground irrigation and such refinements as swimming pool covers will reduce evaporation losses.

Farming will be done with less water too, particularly in areas where the cost is high. We have seen how plastic canopies will turn vast areas into "hothouses" and conserve water that would otherwise return to the atmosphere and blow away. Run-off drainage from a conventional farm is too polluted with salts and other contaminants to be useful for irrigation, but it does sink into the ground and recharge the underground stores of water that supply our wells. The same is true of industrially polluted water. Time was when this was allowed to run back into rivers or lakes and slowly turn them into sticky, smelly messes of no use to anything or anyone. In 2001 scientific engineering practices will screen out pollutants from water to be so returned. Water that cannot economically be treated will be allowed to settle into the ground, where pollutants are removed by the soil at no expense.

Over the years streams and lakes once filthy with man's waste will be cleansed by both man and nature. It will take time, determination and money. Although cheap water will be in short supply, there will be no water shortage.

Many city waterworks in 2001 will recirculate domestic water, using as standard procedure a technique tried in desperation in a Kansas town in 1956. The process will be refined so that the water has no undesirable smell, taste or color. An enlightened public knows that nature's water cycle works in the same way. There is just so much water in the world and it is used over and over.

There will be many grades of water, with the price going up as pollution goes down. A farmer may use water from a river or canal that is not of high enough quality for domestic water. His drainage water may be used again by an industrial plant for a cooling or a flushing operation. Industry will reprocess its water and use it again. Industrial runoff water may be purchased by a municipality, purified and used in its system; or the reverse may be true, with industry purchasing waste water from a domestic waterworks. Such methods as lagoon purification are proving fast, simple and economical.

Multiple use of water will be widespread, with domestic effluent purified to the point that it is suitable for boating, swimming and fishing. It is the old natural principle, with the difference that the "hydrologic cycle" is manmade and much smaller than nature's broad-scale method of operating from ocean to clouds to field to river to ocean again.

But this enlightened reclamation of water will not do the whole job. Waste and pollution did not amount to a fourfold increase in consumption in the old days, so there will still be a large shortage for a growing population geared to more and more water use. It will be necessary to make fresh water from salt water in the sea, or from brackish water wherever it is available.

In general, brackish water is cheaper to purify. The method called dialysis which removes impurities by means of a membrane, is used mostly for smaller quantities of water. A typical installation of this sort might be in a small town that relies on brackish well water. You could drink the stuff if you were dying of thirst, although you wouldn't enjoy it. The water has about three thousand parts per million of salts and other pollutants. The electrodialysis plant produces 600,000 gallons of fresh and sweet water daily to take care of some three thousand residents. Originally most homes had two plumbing systems, one supplying high-quality water for drinking and cooking and another using the brackish water straight for lawn use, bathing and toilet. With a gradual reduction in cost of the fresh water, nearly all have switched to fresh water entirely. The plant is a small modern building handled by one engineer on a standby basis. There are no moving parts in the dialysis plant, and breakdowns seldom occur. When they do, the trouble is easily remedied by replacement of membranes, which are inexpensive and simple to install. The wells are constantly recharged by runoff agricultural water in the area.

Portable dialysis units will be available for use in trailers and campers and on vacation trips to areas where fresh water is not in sufficient supply. Small dialysis units are feasible, but for extensive operations we must look to another method.

Now let's look at a large desalinating plant of the

future, perhaps the largest one in the world, located in southern California and producing a fabulous one billion gallons per day. For many years Los Angeles and then SanSan will reach out farther and farther for the water that was the lifeblood of growth. In the 1930s the longest municipal water system in the world was put in, with water piped nearly three hundred miles from the Colorado River. Bringing in water from the Feather River far to the north will not solve the whole problem, particularly as the northern part of burgeoning SanSan will need water too. Arizona will draw increasingly on the Colorado River water supply, along with other southwest states and Mexico. By 2001 California will get most of her water conveniently from the Pacific Ocean. In fact, all of the states that border a body of salt water will use desalinating plants for much of their supply.

The huge installation on the coast between Los Angeles and Long Beach will be a distillation plant that uses nuclear heat for its operation. Byproduct salt and other minerals will help underwrite the cost of desalination, and the nuclear heat itself will be purchased at reduced cost from the electrical power-plant that is the prime user of the nuclear reactor. In many other parts of the world where there are warm waters to tap, fresh water may be a byproduct of a Sea Thermal Energy plant, along with salts and other minerals removed from the water.

The many agencies of the government concerned with water as a resource will merge long before 2001 to form a Department of Water. Its secretary may be a man with a background of service in the United Nations International Hydrological Decade, completed in

1975. The new department will initiate a nationwide water improvement plan that carefully monitors every subproject in the country and guarantees that our water resources are protected and used to the fullest advantage.

Minerals

With plenty of water, clean air to breathe, and adequate food through conservation and modern technology, man can concentrate more thoughtfully on his other resources. There used to be a joke that the only metal shortage in this country was money. With money an antique carryover from precomputer days, there will be no shortage of metal at all in 2001. One reason is that there will be proportionately less metal used. The same is true of minerals. There was a time when nations were dependent on foreign countries for some of their mineral needs, including diamonds, radioactive materials, lightweight metals for aircraft use, and high-strength elements for steel alloys. In 2001 American engineers will have learned to substitute available materials or to create new ones, many of them synthetics that are stronger, cheaper and more expendable.

Forgetting fossil fuels, which we covered in an earlier chapter, let's look at other minerals that are mined. With the use of nuclear explosives, ores are dug at much less cost than by conventional methods. They are often broken up at the site for cheaper processing, too. New methods make possible the economical use of lower-grade ores, and advanced prospecting methods use aircraft and even orbiting spacecraft, plus sophisticated electronic and electromagnetic instrumentation. Man first discovered helium in the sun. In the moon he will discover mining techniques that will be put to good use not only there on our satellite but back on earth as well.

Beneath the oceans that cover three-fourths of the earth there are three times as many mineral deposits as there are under dry land. For some time we have been exploiting these additional resources to a very slight extent with offshore oil wells. In 2001 we will be mining beneath the sea on a vast scale for oil, gas and minerals. In fact we may be exploiting a treasure in minerals right on the ocean floor, much as the miners of an earlier day found rich nuggets of gold lying on the ground. This prospect has been discussed in the chapter on "inner space."

We have mined the sea itself for some time. Man has extracted salt from the sea for ages, and bromine was first taken from sea water in 1924. During World War II magnesium in large quantities was mined from sea water. One cubic mile of sea water (admittedly a lot!) contains 120 million tons of common salt and another 30 million tons or so of other elements, including 18 million tons of magnesium. There are lesser amounts of such valuable resources as gold, silver, copper, manganese, boron and uranium. Practically every element is found in the sea.

It may be argued that these resources are in very low concentration. For example, getting the 18 million tons of magnesium would mean processing 4 billion tons of water. But natural currents could bring the sea water to the processing plant—a plant perhaps linked with a tidal power scheme or an STE power plant.

Timber

Timber is a natural product that men have continually wasted and destroyed. In 2001 our forests will still be useful and inspiring places, a tribute to the foresight of those charged with guarding this valuable resource. "Farming" techniques and harvesting by advanced methods, including the use of balloons to transport logs, will continue. The elimination of pests, weather control, and advanced firefighting techniques will increase productivity, and more efficient use will be made of all the wood crop. Computerized mills will squeeze out every last usable board foot, and waste will be processed into new products, including food substitutes for animals.

As in the case of food, then, we will have sufficient other natural resources in the year 2001. Fusion power will free much of our fossil fuel supplies for other uses. Conservation will add to the stockpiles, and reclamation will lessen the need for digging into them. We will mine the sea and, if need be, the moon and the planets. Most important, man will no longer be the wanton spoiler of his heritage of mineral and other wealth.

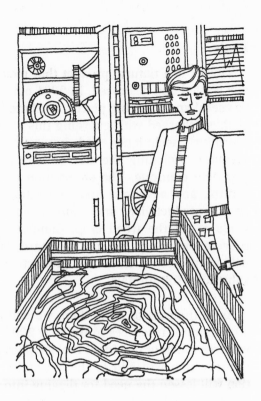

16 Weather

In 2001 we won't talk about the weather so much because we will be doing something about it, contrary to Mark Twain's observation. The weather will be better because man makes it better. This should be little more remarkable than the idea of artificially changing the temperature of our buildings and vehicles. Man has altered "microclimates" for years; in 2001 he will create "macroclimates."

We will control rain, hail, lightning, storms and fog to the benefit of farmer, businessman, sports enthusiast, airman and picknickers. And where we can't control the weather, we will at least know well in advance exactly what is coming so that we can prepare for it.

John von Neumann, one of the pioneers of computer techniques in weather prediction, said that in his opinion accurately foretelling the weather would be every bit as hard as controlling it. By 2001 the computer will permit man to do both. Accurate predictions will come first, aided by the global photographs of world weather transmitted from satellites and then from the moon. With a series of maps made from actual cloud pictures it is fairly easy to see what the general weather will be for some time ahead. Applying computer methods allows meteorologists to make very accurate forecasts for specific areas.

Scientific rainmaking came in 1946, the year that Vincent Schaefer of General Electric sowed pellets of dry ice into a cloud and caused a heavy snowfall. Soon Dr. Irving Langmuir, a Nobel Prize winner, was making it rain out in New Mexico and—so he claimed—all over the country, with just a few pounds of silver iodide! He even believed that he caused a hurricane to swerve from out over the Atlantic and hit the city of Savannah, Georgia, with great damage. The weathermakers of 2001 will routinely turn rain on and off, prevent or weaken storms, pull the teeth of lightning, and protect crops against hail damage.

Let's visit Weather Control Station 12, in the American west. The Headquarters is in Denver, and the primary purpose of the station is to augment the water supply of the Colorado River Basin. Work began back in the 1950s on this project and by 1980, let's say, it had succeeded to the point that the water harvest was increased by forty per cent during an average year. The nerve center of the station is a huge screen showing the entire basin area with its hundreds of seeding points. Remotely controlled, these inject a vapor of tiny particles into the air whenever conditions are right. In summer the result is rain and in winter, snow. Besides the millions of dollars worth of rain added to the reservoirs each year, more millions of dollars will be saved because of floods that are prevented, power outages that don't occur and automobile and plane accidents that don't happen. Forest fires will be prevented by seeding lightning-producing clouds to equalize electrical charges without dangerous bolts of lightning.

Station 12 is typical of hundreds of similar installations all over the world, operating on the same basic principles: careful monitoring of weather conditions, and the measured introduction of seeding materials at just the right times to get the most out of the "rivers in the sky" that constantly carry a tremendous amount of moisture.

In addition to adding water to reservoirs by rainmaking, science in 2001 will keep more of it there by covering the body of water with a film to prevent evaporation. Since this causes the air above the reservoir and downwind of it to be drier than before, here is weather-changing too. An important part of all weathermaking is that each project must be authorized before being put into action. Data fed into computers will show the resulting weather for the area, and nation and the world as a whole from any artificial weather modification. The aim will be not to deprive anyone of rain, or to make him the victim of a flood because of some short-range benefit to another.

A plastic coating on a body of water will prevent fog on land downwind of it, and sheets of plastic placed in the ocean can change the air temperature over it. Such schemes may be used in several localities to alleviate smog conditions along a coast.

Fog Chasing

Our next 2001 stop is an airport, where we can see a demonstration of fog suppression. Schaefer demonstrated this possibility many years ago by whirling a pail of dry ice in the fog and producing a clear pathway when tiny particles of moisture coalesced to form drops large enough to fall out of the air. Dry ice has been used in the United States to clear airports for airliner takeoffs and landings. Orly Field in Paris has used another method—spraying propane into the air from dozens of nozzles located about the airport. The result was the same in both cases: the fog miraculously cleared away. This will probably be the standard method in 2001, and like rainmaking stations it will operate automatically. While the air around the field is blanketed in thick fog, the airport itself and a corridor extending from the runways will be free of fog. The cost is a tiny fraction of the additional revenue from flights not canceled as they once were. Crashes due to fog will be a thing of the past, with a saving of life that cannot be measured in dollars.

Fog suppression will not be limited to airports, of course. Highways also will be kept open for safe driving, as well as seaports and railroad yards. Occasionally a state fair or other extravaganza that depends on clear weather will ask help from the weathermakers and get it.

The Storm-Fighters

Back in the 1800s a device was patented for suppressing tornadoes. It consisted of an explosive charge mounted on a high pole southwest of the "protected" town, to be set off when a tornado approached. The theory was that a tornado usually came from that direction and that the violence of the explosion would rip it apart.

Unfortunately for the inventor and for the victims of tornadoes, the idea didn't work. The course of a tornado is too difficult to predict, and even if it could be intercepted with some sort of a bomb, the amount of energy required to dissipate it would be great. The average tornado would require a nuclear bomb to blast it out of the sky, and the result would be worse than letting the storm run its course! Work is under way toward controlling temperatures at various levels with precipitation or clouds, and thus preventing the inversions that seem to lead to unstable air, which favors tornadoes. Strangely enough, control of hurricanes—far larger than any tornado—will be accomplished first.

Dr. Langmuir died believing that he had altered the course of a hurricane in 1947. Many meteorologists were just as convinced he had nothing to do with it or the rainfall he seemed to have induced in the east with his western cloud seeding. But for years the Government persevered with hurricane-busting attempts.

Before 2001, success will come. Computer studies and moving pictures of the formation of hurricanes will lead to the same sort of breakthrough in abating their force that was achieved by special cloud seeding for reducing the amount of lightning.

Before a hurricane really has time to get started, while it is still close to the Equator, fast airplanes will bombard its clouds with rockets carrying seeding material. Hundreds, even thousands, of such shots will be required, skilfully placed just where they will do the most good. It is water that gives the storm its energy; when a hurricane moves over land it dissipates relatively quickly. By causing most of the water to precipitate as rain, weather control will weaken the storm before it can gain the momentum that leads to gale winds. The stormbusters will not—perhaps ever—be one hundred per cent effective, for even with computers it is terribly difficult to plot all the complexities of huge storms. But even fifty per cent will be a good percentage, and many of the storms that do form and swing north will be far weaker and shorter-lived than those of earlier years. Equally important, careful records will be kept to see that hurricane-busting has no adverse affects on other global weather. For instance, if it should be found that because hurricanes are stopped torrential rains flood England and Europe or temperatures drop on the American coast-line, storm-fighting may prove a risk not worth the gamble.

Climates to Order

Long ago Russia suggested warming the Arctic seas to make Siberia a better place to live and farm. By

2001 there may be carefully controlled experiments in the frozen north with nuclear reactors sunk to the bottom of the sea, where they will warm the water slowly. Ice floes and snow on land will be dusted with fine carbon black for faster melting. In time the surface water and also that of the land will be warm.

More complex schemes may be tried in several tropical areas to learn if pleasanter temperatures can be produced on land. Here the sea will be cooled slightly by running a huge sea thermal energy plant for years in one location, slowly cooling the surface water with water from far beneath the surface. Even if the climate-changing part of the program doesn't work, the project will pay off because of the power generated for a new industrial area on shore.

Long ago, scientists learned that islands caused "thermal" currents in the atmosphere that in turn produced clouds. Weathermakers will create such vertical air currents artificially by using asphalt or other black material to absorb heat from the sun instead of reflecting it. Air heated by conduction, will rise and condense to produce cumulus clouds. The result will be precipitation if conditions are just right. By reversing this technique, the weathermakers will reduce clouds and rain by creating large areas of reflective surface instead of heat-soaking terrain. The result will be better farming and better resort weather because of more sunshine.

Climate-changing projects may be undertaken where regions have been nonproductive dust bowls, with dust particles trapped in the air and constantly increasing as more dust is blown from the parched surface below. Such regions will be irrigated and seeded so that vegetation comes back. This is a costly process and cannot be continued indefinitely, but it will not have to be. As the dust is removed from the air, rainfall will increase, since fewer but larger droplets will form. And with more rain there will be more vegetation and still more rain. The rains that originally blessed the area will return and will continue.

There is another side to the weather control coin. It was mentioned earlier that man has inadvertently changed the weather in years past, dustbowls being a tragic example. Manmade smog is another. In southern California, ozone reacts with sunlight to make the smog problem far worse. Elimination of ozone and other pollutants will result in skies that are as blue in 2001 as they were when Hollywood became the Mecca of moviemakers.

Weathermaking with a Vengeance

When General Electric's legal staff learned that Vincent Schaefer had made it snow they were horrified. That was the last weather experimenting the firm did; its projects were all turned over to the Government! Weathermaking law is even more complex and confused than water law, which was probably the worst kind until it was learned that man could tamper with the clouds and make or suppress rain, hail, fog and lightning. By 2001 there will be a great background of case law on the subject and few legal problems. In our rivers in the sky there is ample moisture for everyone without depriving the man downwind of his share. The only time that might occur would be in wartime, when weathermaking would surely be called into play as a weapon.

Fog suppression was first used in England during

World War II so that the RAF could defend the island against the Nazis. It was used again by the U. N. forces in Korea. The first intentional *creation* of fog in wartime could come in a small "brushfire" operation, with an invading force trapped in mountainous country for several days by manmade white stuff.

It is to be hoped that nothing worse in the way of weathermaking is ever necessary when men set out against each other in anger, for far more potent ideas have been dreamed up. Rain might be made to flood an enemy, and drought to starve him out. Here would be a scorched-earth policy carried out with nothing more than the sun shining down unmercifully day after day, month after month, to burn up crops and melt away water supplies. And men who can knock out a hurricane might be able to start one up on demand and steer it to where it would do the most good against an enemy. Weather moves about the world in an unending circle. In peacetime all nations are careful what they do to their good neighbors downwind, but the idea can be reversed in wartime.

There will be some truly colossal projects on the weathermaking drawing board in 2001, although they will most likely not be tried until the world is in desperate condition. By adding CO_2 to the atmosphere, for example, more heat can be trapped. By altering the radiation belts—on a larger scale than was done long ago with nuclear space blasts—the amount of energy reaching earth from the sun can be altered. It is known, for example, that the jet streams, those high-altitude, high-speed rivers of air, are shifted drastically when solar radiation fluctuates. And it has been learned that our weather is geared to the jet-stream movement. Many years ago Dr. C. G. Abbot showed that sunspots affect our weather. If we change incoming solar radiation of a certain kind, we may drastically change weather all over the world—just how remains to be seen. It is not a project to be entered into lightly.

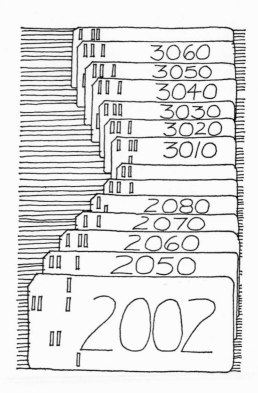

17 The Unexpected

To this point our look at what awaits us in the year 2001 has been a more or less straight-line extension of past to present to future. Even this simple approach yields a tomorrow that beckons temptingly with a promise of a life that is better and more interesting by far than the remarkable one we now lead. But what of the unexpected? What revolutionary findings are to be added to our trove of treasure by 2001? Electricity was stumbled onto by Luigi Galvani when he noticed the strange twitching of dismembered frog's legs in his laboratory. Penicillin was discovered when a nurse made a bad mistake and left open the window of a hospital laboratory. Cryobiology came of age when jars of honey and glycerin were accidentally mixed in experiments. Ceramic glass wasn't planned, but happened when not one but three mistakes occurred in another laboratory. Success in rainmaking came by chance when Schaefer sought to cool down his freezer, which had warmed up during lunch hour when he left it open. Nobody was looking for X rays or gamma rays when they were found. Wohler synthesized urea entirely by chance.

A generation ago there were no predictions of electronic computers or communications satellites. No prognosticators suggested that nuclear energy would be a major weapon of war and peace in a few decades. The laser wasn't dreamed of, and neither was holography. Transistors and solar batteries came quickly and by surprise. Photography and sound recording were unexpected inventions. It would be well, then, to make some allowance for a number of unexpected developments in the next three decades. This allowance must be general, however, and about all we can say is that several tremendous advances will have as much impact as computers, nuclear energy and radio.

Some of the surprises may well be the final realization of age-old dreams and schemes toward which men have plotted and planned for hundreds and even thousands of years. Let's consider a few of these that man has long sought.

Invisibility has thus far escaped the inventor and remains the property of science-fiction writers alone. Just how useful this will be is questionable, except for spies who might still have employment. Of course, for camouflaging necessary industrial and domestic structures, such as water tanks and bracings for buildings, invisibility would be an answer. In 1989 a young physicist, researching the properties of various materials as lasers, may be surprised to find part of his equipment suddenly disappear, only to come back into view when he switches off the pulse current to a new organic polymer he has been testing. Repeated experiments show that the new material has the weird property of acting as a lens that causes light to bend around objects in the vicinity. Here is invisibility, at last!

An even stranger discovery might come in 1992, this one a result of programed serendipity. Simulation studies on a new method of catalyzing chemicals in the manufacture of plastics for the textile industry may suggest that atoms are being polarized, much as light can be by certain lenses. Directed research produces solid materials with a specific gravity nearly that of water, yet capable of passing through one another like so much air or smoke!

What could you do with structures that could merge with one another and separate with no change in them? For one thing, you could store a hundred of them in the space formerly occupied by only one. And if one were a vehicle and the other a garage you wouldn't need a door. The possibilities are endless, especially when it is learned that living tissue may be so catalyzed that it too becomes permeable.

Antigravity has eluded the inventor in spite of some

high-level research toward finding weightless substances. The best man has done is to overcome gravity with such devices as rockets, airplane engines and trampolines, yet there seems to be some connection between electricity and magnetism and gravity. We can protect against the first two forces, so why not the last? And when someone succeeds, what will be the practical applications, besides space flight—weightless building materials; a flying suit that will really be that; a bicycle that will coast up hill? Perhaps our ingenuity, or that of the computer, can find ways to put antigravity to work. Da Vinci gave up on perpetual motion, as have most intelligent people since, yet in the late 1960s a British scientist suggested that one day it just might be achieved. However, with fusion power or some other such exotic power supply, who would need perpetual motion?

How about a matter transmitter? Perhaps all we need is an efficient matter *converter*. Energy and matter are different manifestations of the same thing: matter is frozen energy, to put it one way. Suppose someone develops a transmitter of electromagnetic energy that is fed by putting blocks of metal into it. A receiver out in space or on Mars picks up the waves and reconverts them into metal. The result would be high-speed transportation. It does not seem probable that spacecraft in the near future will travel at anything like the speed of light, but the matter transmitter gets around this difficulty neatly. Now, having converted a block of aluminum, how about trying an organic material like wood? And if that works, a living thing like a virus or a bacterium or an amoeba or a mouse. Or a man.

Much work has been done with dolphins, and Dr.

John C. Lilly is convinced that they have intelligence approaching that of man. Why not more communication between man and animal? Why not teach intelligent animals to work for us and with us for food gathering, transportation, and household service?

Mental telepathy cannot be demonstrated conclusively enough to satisfy the scientist, but success may come by 2001. Of all possibilities, this one may have the greatest impact on society. With communication between minds no longer filtered, garbled, muted or muffled in any way, surely we would begin to know and understand each other better.

Transmutation, the changing of one element into another, has been achieved. Man has even changed energy to matter and matter to energy, a transmutation the alchemists did not even hope for, but what of routinely changing any element into any other—say, lead to radium, instead of vice versa as nature does it? Presently it would seem that this could be done only with an expenditure of energy more costly than the increase in value between lead and the more precious element, but there may be a trick or two the physicist will learn. Deuterium is an example. This heavy water differs from ordinary water by a cost factor of millions but only by a slight atomic difference. Nature produces a few such isotopes in her own good time, but maybe man can mechanize the process. It may even prove possible and feasible to create elements from scratch, building with protons and neutrons and electrons— again, the way nature does it but with variations to suit our own theme.

The dream of creating giants or midgets persists from old fairy tales. Suppose someone stumbles onto, or consciously develops, a matter shrinker or stretcher that will change a model airplane into one big enough to carry passengers, or a six-foot man into a six-inch version for a special mission into space? All that is involved is a few details like molecular attraction and gravity.

There are medical discoveries that would be welcomed by many. That cure for the common cold for example—or for baldness or gray hair. Or a simple control for height, weight and facial features. There might be an elixir of life to restore to us the promise of Ponce de Leon's Fountain of Youth—or another elixir that would make us as wise as Solomon, Einstein and Shakespeare all in one, simply by transferring the genetic codes of the brightest intellects of our time. In addition to the smart pill there might be a happy pill as good as the soma of Huxley's "Brave New World."

For ages men have patronized fortune-tellers, clairvoyants and seers, yet in the computer we may have a far more accurate fortune-teller for the years ahead. Certainly as its memory capacity increases, and as better prediction programs are worked out by computers for computers, we will be given printouts forecasting population and economy and weather and war and just about anything else we want to know.

How about a new transportation method? (Before you say there cannot be any not yet thought of, consider the air-car or the Levitrain, which sprang up from nowhere.) How about a new form of entertainment that will be to television what television was to radio and what radio was to the gramophone? What will we find as we bore deeper into the earth, as we shall continue to do? Will man capture small asteroids and mine them for the precious minerals they possess, or even turn them into huge spaceships on which to explore the galaxy? President Johnson predicted the first possibility in 1962; by 2001 both may have come to pass.

The Bad Possibilities

Since we are all basically optimistic, this book has been written with the thought that the changes we will find in 2001 will all be for the good. Little mention has been made of the horrors of war, disease, natural catastrophes, or invasion by men from other worlds intent on killing or subjugating us. The possibility that some apparently beneficial discovery might turn into a terrible curse, such as a drug for cancer that also renders us all sterile or doomed to die horribly within ten years of such treatment. These things could happen; we get no guarantee that life will all be good when we come to this planet.

Nuclear energy has been described as giving us untold power, including beneficial radiation for medical and other purposes, desalination and space travel. It can also blow us all to kingdom come—or, worse yet, horribly mutilate or mutate us. Like the terrible drug suggested, radiation might also render us sterile. Nuclear energy could conceivably finally start that chain reaction dreaded by scientists and laymen in the 1940s. Or it might poison the environment and render it unlivable for ages into the future.

The colonization of the moon could turn into a military operation aimed at severing contact with earth, with nuclear war ensuing to the harm of one or the other or both parties. A mission to Jupiter or Saturn or

Mars might bring back a terrible plague that wipes out humanity in short order. Or genetic monsters created by well-meaning biochemists in the test tube might threaten society.

The weather changers, after years of blessing mankind, may prove to have wrecked the atmosphere and turned it into a trap for radiation or gases or pollutants that slowly sicken us or kill us off. Taken up as a war measure, weather control could be a horrible affair, leading to flood, fire and famine, to say nothing of raging winds and extremes of temperature that could make life unbearable.

Even our vaunted computerized world may prove a terrible enemy in disguise. What would happen if such a system were to break down and not be repairable for a year or so? Could man, unaccustomed to using his own brains, manage to hold things together for six billion souls?

Time will tell, but if we reach 2001 at all the odds are in our favor that we will reach a better world. During all natural history, the direction seems to have been toward something better. And for those who complain of their lot, it is often helpful to ask if they would like to trade with their ancestors of a hundred years since. Or fifty years, or even twenty.

The writer lives in a world he considers better than that of his parents. He is sure that 2001 will offer his children a pleasanter and more rewarding maturity than was his. In fact, he realizes with some envy the fact that when the happy year arrives he will not be as young as he is now.

Index

computer: in banking, 15, 58, 61; as enemy, 175; games with, 17; in global government, 30; in government, 27-28; in highway construction, 58-60; in home, 11, 15; human rights and, 65-66; industry and, 84; intelligence of, 57; in medicine, 61-62, 123; memory of, 62-63; music from, 12, 97; in preschool education, 69-70; science and, 111-115; in space flight, 102; in traffic, 36-37; various uses of, 5-7, 47, 56-66; in weather control, 163
copying machines, 84
Cousteau, Jacques-Yves, 105
credit cards, 3, 84
credit machines, 85
crime prevention and control, 28-29
cryobiology, 169
cryogenic suspended animation, 5, 101, 121
cultured steak, 133
culture farming, 132-134
cybernation, 7, 81-82
Cylert, 79

Darwin, Charles, 113
deep freeze, 121; for space travel, 101
desalination, 4, 127; solar energy and, 141
desalination plant, 153-155
deuterium, 145, 172
dialysis, of water, 153-154
dirt farming, 126-127
disease, elimination of, 122-123
dishwater, automatic, 13
Disneyland, 7, 94
diving, motorized, 107; see also skindiving
dolphins, 171
door-opener, 11
drug addiction, 97-98, 117
drugs, in learning, 6, 79, 117; in

warfare, 32
dust bowls, 164-165

education, 67-79; goals of, 71-72; see also learning
Einstein, Albert, 111, 173
elections, by computer, 27-28
Electoral College, 27
electric automobile, 5, 35-38, 149; fuel and, 136-137
electric home, 7, 14-15; see also home
electricity, power supply and, 142-144; solar, 14
electric meter, billing from, 15
electromagnetic waves, 45
electronic eavesdropping, 49
electronic housekeeper, 7, 136
electrostatic precipitators, 11-12
English language, as world language, 5, 51
ENIAC, 63
ersatz food, 132
Esperanto, 51
extrasensory perception, 54

fallout, 16
family income, 7, 89-90
farming, 83-84; dirt, 126-127; fish, 107, 129; mechanization of, 126-127; population and, 125-126; in water, 127-129
filling station, demise of, 148-149
fish farming, 107, 129
floor covering, 11
flying suit, 171
fog: creation of, 165; suppression or chasing of, 161-162, 165-166
food, 124-134; supplements and substitutes for, 130-132
food additives, 129
food center, home, 12
food pills, 125
food preservation, 13
fossil fuels, 132, 138, 143, 155
Fountain of Youth, 173

Franklin, Benjamin, 46, 50
freeway, driverless cars on, 36
fuel, fossil, *see* fossil fuels: power and, 135-146; transportation and, 136-137
fuel cell, 14, 31, 35-36, 142-143, 150
"fun cities," 97
fusion power, 4, 144-145, 157

Galvani, Luigi, 169
gambling, 97
gasoline engine, obsolescence of, 5
General Electric Company, 159, 165
genetic mutations, 122, 175
geothermal wells, 139
giants, creation of, 172-173
gills, for humans, 93, 106
glass walls, electronic, 12
global business, 87-88
golf, 92
government, 23-33; computers in, 57; local, 25
Gross National Product, 8, 88

health, 61-62, 116-123
heart transplants, 118-119
heavy water, 145, 172
helicopter, 5
helium, 156
highway construction, computers and, 58-59
highway fatalities, 37
holography, 8, 47
home: computer in, 11-12, 14-16; "house power" of, 21; lifetime of, 19; materials for, 16; of 1930's, 19-20; of 1960's, 20; robot servants in, 7, 136; size of, 18; technical and architectural features of, 10-22
horse, as transportation, 35
housecleaning, 15, 22
hovercraft, 43
human conduct, 8
hunting, 83

hurricanes, control of, 162
Huxley, Aldous, 173
hydroelectric plant, solar energy and, 141-142
hydrogen bomb, 32
hydrologic cycle, 152
hypersonic transport (HST), 5, 40-41
hypothermia, 121; space travel and, 101

industrial pollution, 149-150
industry: education in, 72; occupations in, 83-84
information retrieval, 113
inner space, 105-108
integrated circuits, 64
Internal Revenue Service, 48, 66
invisibility, 170
irrigation, 14

Johnson, Lyndon B., 174

kidney, artificial, 120
"kilowatt karts," 149; *see also* electric car

Langmuir, Irving, 159, 162
language, global communications and, 51-53
large-scale integration, 64
laser, 7; invisibility and, 170; in space travel, 104; telephony and, 48-49
laser death ray, 32
law enforcement, 26-28
learning: drugs and, 79; programed, 6; transfer of, 78-79; *see also* education
leisure time, 17, 21
Leon, Ponce de, 173
Levitrain, 173
library, by computer, 16; school, 68
life expectancy, 117-118
light: speed of, 48; speeds faster than, 50

INDEX

INDEX

THE AUTHOR

D. S. HALACY, JR., a South Carolinian by birth, was educated in California and Arizona and worked in the aircraft industry before serving the Air Force as a navigator and radar observer during World War II and the Korean War. After successive terms as engineering writer for AiResearch, chief editor for Goodyear Aircraft and manager of the Motorola Technical Information Center, he devoted his full attention to writing and has published more than 40 books including both fiction and nonfiction.

Mr. Halacy, a veteran at interpreting science for young people, lives with his wife and two daughters in Arizona, and in 1966 had the distinction of being elected a state senator.